Mind and Machine

Exploring the Analogies between the Human Brain and Artificial Intelligence

Amol R. Madane

Amol R. Madane
1st Edition

Publication Date: August 2024
Price: ₹799 | $ 15
ISBN: *978-93-5847-287-5*
Published by:
Adhyyan Books
Office No. 125,
Opposite Vivanta by Taj,
DDA SFS. Pocket-1, Dwarka,
Sec-22, New Delhi-110077
Website: http://adhyyanbooks.com
E-mail: contact@adhyyanbooks.com

Printed at: Repro Printers, Delhi

Contents

Overview of the Book

Purpose and Target Audience

"Mind and Machine: Exploring the Analogies between the Human Brain and Artificial Intelligence" is a painstakingly produced book intended to close the knowledge gap between two complex disciplines: artificial intelligence (AI) and neuroscience. With an emphasis on the engineering field, this book seeks to improve knowledge of the complexity of the human brain and how they could motivate and guide the creation of AI technology. Professionals already working in the many engineering disciplines as well as undergraduate and graduate engineering students make up the main readership for this book. Though they might not be very knowledgeable about neuroscience or artificial intelligence, these people usually have a strong basis in technological ideas. This group will consequently find the content enlightening, enhancing their technical and practical abilities with knowledge from the sophisticated operations of the human brain. The book tries to develop a better knowledge of how neural mechanisms might guide and progress AI applications by emphasising parallels between the brain and AI. This is especially helpful to people working in domains where integrating several disciplines is becoming more and more important, such robotics, machine learning, and computational neuroscience.

Scope and Structure

With an emphasis on applications and consequences in engineering, the book is organised to offer a thorough investigation of the connection between neuroscience and artificial intelligence. Every chapter is intended to gradually increase the audience's knowledge by fusing ethical issues and real-world situations with theoretical underpinnings.

Beginnings of Neuroscience and Artificial Intelligence This chapter introduces engineers to the fundamental ideas of neuroscience, therefore setting the scene. Examining the development of AI from its beginnings to the present, it concentrates on significant turning points that are relevant to comprehending its potential and constraints. Furthermore covered in this chapter is the need of making comparisons between AI systems and the human brain, therefore laying the groundwork for later chapters.

Neurones and Artificial Neurones, Chapter 2 The emphasis of this chapter moves to a thorough comparison of artificial and biological neurons. The architectures of artificial neural networks that neurons inspire are examined together with their structure and function. This includes a direct comparison of the mechanics of learning and activation functions in AI systems with biological processes.

In Chapter 3, Brain Connectivity and Neural Networks Neural network architecture is contrasted with the connection observed in the human brain. Drawing analogies to the structure and operation of engineered systems, this chapter uses ideas from network resilience and graph theory. Additionally covered are the significance of hierarchical organisation and parallel processing in biological systems as well as in industrial applications.

Learning and Memory, Chapter 4 Here, we discuss learning mechanisms in artificial intelligence and biological systems. The chapter compares and contrasts the several AI learning algorithms—supervised and unsupervised—with biological learning processes. This comparison demonstrates how computers learn and offers understanding of memory systems and how engineering solutions reflect these ideas.

An Artificial General Intelligence (AGI) and Consciousness Chapter 5 The intricate subjects of consciousness and artificial intelligence are introduced in this chapter. The difficulties and moral issues raised by building robots that might eventually mimic human consciousness are covered. Explored is the search for artificial intelligence, emphasising the significant consequences of such developments as well as the technical obstacles.

Cognitive Functions and AI Applications, Chapter 6 Here the emphasis is on applications of AI in engineering tasks that simulate human cognitive processes. This encompasses in machines emotional intelligence, decision-making, and perception. Additionally covered is how AI might revolutionise conventional engineering methods by promoting creativity and innovation in engineering ideas.

Issues and Prospects for the Future chapter 7 The present problems in fusing artificial intelligence (AI) with neuroscience and engineering are covered in the last chapter. Technical obstacles are covered, as is the necessity of strong regulation and ethical issues. Examining the prospects of AI in engineering as the chapter comes to an end, the need of multidisciplinary cooperation and creativity is emphasised. Those who are involved with the material should at the end of this book have a thorough grasp of how neuroscience discoveries can significantly impact AI development, particularly in engineering settings. The book is meant to educate as well as to stimulate fresh concepts and inventions that push the limits of what machines are capable of.

1
Foundations of Neuroscience and AI

1.1 Introduction to Neuroscience

Neuroscience is a rich and expansive field that delves into the complexities of the nervous system, which orchestrates a range of functions from the simplest reflexes to sophisticated cognitive processes. This interdisciplinary science draws on the principles of various fields such as biology, chemistry, psychology, and medicine to explore how neurons operate both in states of health and disease.

At its core, neuroscience seeks to understand the mechanisms of neural function, shedding light on the processes that underlie human thought, emotion, and behavior. This understanding is critical not just in the realm of medicine and healthcare but increasingly so in fields like artificial intelligence (AI) and engineering, where insights into neural function are informing new technologies and systems.

The nervous system is built from cells called neurons, which are the primary units of brain function. There are approximately 86 billion neurons in the human brain, each intricately connected to thousands of others through networks that form the physical basis of our thoughts, memories, and perceptions. Neurons are exceptionally diverse in function and form, but they share some common structures that are crucial for their role in transmitting information.

Each neuron consists of a cell body (soma), dendrites, and an axon. The cell body contains the nucleus and cytoplasm, serving as the control center of the neuron, where most protein synthesis occurs. Dendrites branch out from the cell body and act like antennae, receiving chemical signals from other neurons. The axon, often much longer than dendrites, extends from the cell body and specializes in transmitting these electrical signals to other neurons or to muscles, facilitating communication across the distances within the body.

This communication between neurons occurs at synapses, the specialized junctions where the axon tip of one neuron meets a dendrite or cell body of another. Synaptic transmission is the process by which neurons communicate with each other, involving the release of molecules called neurotransmitters. These neurotransmitters cross the synaptic gap to bind to receptor sites on a neighboring neuron, thereby influencing whether that neuron will generate a similar electrical impulse.

Understanding neurotransmission is crucial for engineers and AI professionals as it provides a model of efficient information processing that can inspire the development of artificial neural networks. These networks aim to mimic the brain's ability to quickly and effectively process vast amounts of information through complex networks of interconnected nodes, which are analogous to biological neurons.

Moreover, the study of how neurons adapt their connections during learning—known as synaptic plasticity—offers invaluable insights into how systems can improve over time. This principle is central to machine learning, where algorithms adjust and optimize their operations based on new data, much like how synaptic connections strengthen or weaken in response to learning and memory formation.

The relevance of neuroscience to engineering extends beyond the emulation of brain architecture into more practical applications. For instance, understanding sensory processing in the nervous system can help in designing better sensors and interfaces for robotic systems, allowing them to interact with their environment in more sophisticated and intuitive ways. Similarly, insights into neural pathways involved in decision-making and problem-solving can lead to algorithms that better mimic human reasoning, potentially making machines not just faster, but more adaptable and seemingly intuitive.

Thus, neuroscience does not just inform AI and engineering with models to replicate; it provides a framework for questioning and redefining what is possible in technology. By exploring the foundational aspects of neural structure and function, professionals in these fields can unlock new potentials in computing and robotics, paving the way for innovations that could transform how we interact with machines and how machines interpret the world.

1.2 Evolution of AI

Theevolution of artificial intelligence (AI) from its conceptual birth to itscurrent status as a transformational force in a variety of industries is bothfascinating and educational. Since the mid-twentieth century, AI has evolvedfrom simple theoretical constructs to complex systems capable of doingactivities previously assumed to be solely human.

The origins of AI as a formal subject may be traced back to the 1950s, a timeof significant advances in computing capacity and theoretical understanding.The phrase "artificial intelligence" was coined by John McCarthy in1956 at the Dartmouth Conference, which is widely regarded as the beginning ofAI as an autonomous field. This era paved the way for early experiments like asAlan Turing's work, which argued that machines could replicate human intellect,and the Turing Test as an intelligence criteria.

In its early years, AI research was largely concerned with developingprogrammes capable of doing specific tasks such as chess or algebraic problems.These early AI systems followed a set of rules and logic to solve issues in acontrolled setting. For example, IBM's Deep Blue, a chess-playing computer,famously defeated reigning world champion Garry Kasparov in 1997, indicatingthat machines may match or even outperform humans in certain specific skills.

However, with the introduction of machine learning in the late twentiethcentury, the scope of AI began to broaden substantially. Machine learning, asubset of AI, is the creation of algorithms that enable computers to learn fromand make judgements based on data. This transition from hard-coded instructionsto systems that can learn from experience was a watershed milestone in thegrowth of AI.

The emergence of neural networks, inspired by the neural architecture of thehuman brain, catapulted AI to new heights. These networks, made up of layers ofinterconnected nodes (or "neurons"), enabled robots to process datain complicated ways, resulting in advances in pattern recognition and dataanalysis. This feature proved particularly beneficial in industries such asfinance, where AI systems could recognise trends and make forecasts based onpast data, and healthcare, where they could help diagnose diseases by analysingmedical images.

Deep learning, a sophisticated form of machine learning that employs deepneural networks, has recently been at the forefront of AI advances. Deeplearning trains models to make highly accurate predictions and judgements byutilising vast amounts of data and significant computational power. Thistechnology has contributed significantly to the advancement of natural languageprocessing (NLP), allowing computers to interpret and synthesise human languagewith great sophistication. Chatbots, translation services, and voice-activatedassistants are already commonplace as a result of these improvements.

Furthermore, robotics has incorporated artificial intelligence to developmachines that can interact with their surroundings in ways that imitate humanactions. AI-enabled robots may learn from their surroundings and executeactivities ranging from assembly line work to sophisticated surgery,dramatically increasing precision and efficiency.

As AI advances, its incorporation into daily life and numerous professionaldomains grows. Understanding AI's historical history is critical forengineering professionals not just to appreciate its current applications, butalso to envisage future developments. This historical backdrop highlights AI'stransformational potential, as well as the issues it poses, such as ethicalconcerns, the need for regulation, and the societal ramifications of autonomoussystems.

Reflecting on the growth of AI, it is evident that what began as a quest todiscover whether robots could think has evolved into a broader investigation ofhow AI may improve human talents and revolutionise sectors. This continualevolution promises not just to push the bounds of technology, but also to callinto question our core notions of what it is to be human in an increasinglycomputerised society.

1.3 Comparative Analysis

When we consider how the human brain functions andcompare it to artificial intelligence (AI) systems, we uncover a wealth ofinsights. For example, our brains process information with remarkableefficiency, using minimal energy. This feat of natural engineering is somethingAI researchers aim to replicate through neuromorphic computing. Neuromorphicsystems utilize designs inspired by the brain's own architecture, leading tomore energy-efficient and capable machines.

The brain also excels at parallel processing,managing multiple tasks at once with ease. In contrast, traditional computershave often worked sequentially, handling one task at a time. Recognizing this,developers have created parallel processing technologies, like GPUs. These areessential in fields requiring quick computation and large data handling, suchas video processing and complex scientific simulations.

Moreover, the brain's ability to learn from just afew examples is extraordinary. This process, known as synaptic plasticity,involves the strengthening or weakening of connections between neurons based onthe frequency and type of signals passed between them. This ability is a sourceof inspiration for AI, leading to the development of algorithms that improvetheir accuracy and efficiency with less data, which is crucial for applicationsin environments where data is scarce or expensive to obtain.

1.4 Importance of Analogies

The practice of drawing analogies between the humanbrain and AI systems extends beyond academic exploration. It has concreteapplications in technology development, especially in AI and engineering. Theseanalogies offer a blueprint for designing machines that emulate the biologicalefficiency and adaptability of the human brain. For example, understanding howthe brain learns and remembers has spurred the creation of innovative AIalgorithms and structures that mimic these cognitive processes.

These analogies also foster interdisciplinarycollaboration, uniting engineers, neuroscientists, and AI researchers. Thiscollaboration enriches AI development, grounding cutting-edge technology innatural processes. Such cross-disciplinary work is crucial as it blends diverseinsights and approaches, leading to robust and scalable innovations. Theseadvancements often mimic human cognitive processes more closely, making themmore intuitive and effective.

Through understanding and applying the principlesobserved in the human brain, AI technology not only advances but also becomesmore aligned with natural, human-like processing. This approach doesn't justsolve technical problems—it revolutionizes how we interact with technology,making it more responsive, intuitive, and capable in complex environments. Theintegration of these fields continues to push the boundaries of what machinescan do, opening up new possibilities for future innovations that couldtransform our daily lives.

1.5 Overview of the Book

This book is structured to guide the reader through a progressive exploration of both neuroscience and artificial intelligence. The subsequent chapters build on the foundation laid here, delving deeper into specific areas of interest:

- **Chapter 2: Neurons and Artificial Neurons** explores the detailed architecture of biological neurons and their artificial counterparts, providing the reader with a granular understanding of how neural information processing is mirrored in AI systems.

- **Chapter 3: Neural Networks and Brain Connectivity** examines the structural and functional similarities between biological neural networks and artificial neural networks, with a focus on how these structures can be optimized for various engineering applications.

- **Chapter 4: Learning and Memory** discusses the mechanisms of learning and memory in the brain and how these concepts have been adapted to enhance machine learning technologies.

- **Chapter 5: Consciousness and Artificial General Intelligence (AGI)** tackles more abstract concepts such as consciousness and the pursuit of AGI, analyzing both the technological and ethical dimensions of these endeavours.

- **Chapter 6: Cognitive Functions and AI Applications** looks at practical applications of AI in replicating or augmenting human cognitive functions, such as perception, decision-making, and emotional intelligence.

- **Chapter 7: Challenges and Future Directions** addresses the current limitations and future opportunities in the integration of AI with neuroscience, emphasizing the need for continued innovation and ethical considerations.

By the end of this book, engineering professionals and students will have a comprehensive understanding of how insights from neuroscience can be leveraged to advance artificial intelligence, enriching their work in the engineering field with innovative approaches and cutting-edge technologies.

2

Neurons and Artificial Neurons

2.1 Neurons' Anatomy

The neuron is the cell of the nerve, and it is considered the basic machinery for all body functions, both cognitive and physical, that function together. The neuron is a basic unit of both the brain and the entire nervous system. The neurons deliver electric information and some chemical signals that are circulating through the body. Typically, a neuron consists of three basic structural constituents: a cell body (or soma), dendrites, and an axon. The cell body has a nucleus, which in turn has the genetic material of the neuron and nuclear material able to organize metabolic activities within the neuron. Most of the organelles found within the cytoplasm are within the cytoplasm of the cell body. Such organelles that are in the cytoplasm include mitochondria that provide energy for various activities within the neuron, and ribosomes, which produce proteins necessary for the function and structure of a neuron. Actually, the dendrites are more or less tube-like branches, seemingly reminiscent of the tree. In every detail, it is for the sake of communicating with other neurons. They have synapses all over them, which are points of contact where signals from axons of other neurons are received. Each neuron has from one to thousands of dendrites, which go to greatly increase the surface area and capacity for information processing.

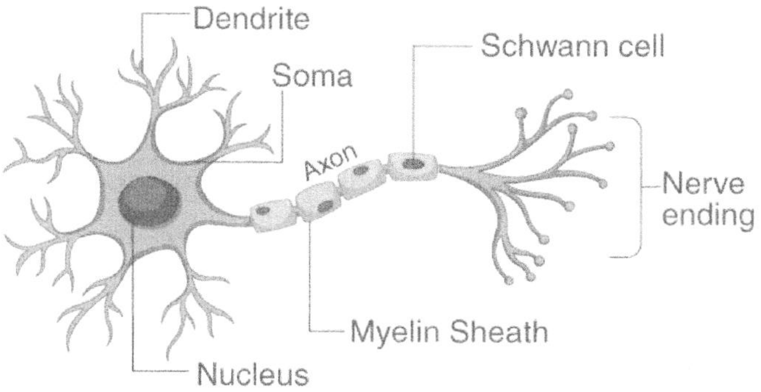

Figure 2.1: Anatomy of a Neuron

This figure provides a detailed illustration of a neuron, the fundamental unit of the nervous system responsible for transmitting information.

- ***Cell Body (Soma):*** *The cell body, labeled in Figure 2.1, is the central part of the neuron and contains the nucleus, which houses the genetic material, and other organelles essential for the neuron's function.*

- ***Dendrites:*** *Branching out from the cell body are dendrites (also labeled in Figure 2.1). These are responsible for receiving signals from other neurons.*

- ***Axon:*** *A single, long fiber called the axon (labeled in Figure 2.1) emerges from the cell body. The axon transmits electrical signals away from the neuron to other cells.*

- ***Myelin Sheath:*** *Some axons are wrapped in a fatty substance called the myelin sheath (labeled in Figure 2.1). This insulation speeds up the transmission of electrical signals.*

• ***Synapse:*** *The synapse (labeled in Figure 2.1) is the junction point where the axon of one neuron meets the dendrite or cell body of another neuron. It's the site where chemical messengers (neurotransmitters) are released and received, enabling communication between neurons.*

The axon arises from the soma and is a long, thin projection capable of reaching more than a meter in length in humans, transmitting electrical impulses away from the cell body of the neuron onto other neurons, muscles, or glands. Axons differ in length and branch, contacting many cells. Myelin sheaths, generally covering the axons, are composed of fatty substances that insulate and greatly speed the electrical transmission. For instance, in the periphery nervous system, axons of the motor neurons can extend from the spinal cord to all the muscles of the feet, showing the incredible length that some axons are capable of.

The synaptic transmission is an important part of the communication that takes place between neurons at synapses—specialized junctions through which two neurons communicate with each other. The passing of electrical impulse, otherwise known as action potential, to the axon terminal triggers the release of neurotransmitters. After that, the chemical messengers go through the synaptic gap and mix with receptor sites on the postsynaptic neuron. In its turn, it may bring activation or inhibition of postsynaptic neuron, thus effectively controlling impulse transmission in this part of the body.

Effective and perfect speed of synaptic transmission is obligatory for the synthesis of some complex behaviors and functions. For instance, driving at high speed requires the rapid process of information pertaining to sensory motor responses. Other neurotransmitters involved—the set just as well—dopamine and serotonin play almost equal roles not only in the motor control but also in the regulation of mood and the process of making decisions.

Another cornerstone of neuronal function is synaptic plasticity, the ability for synapses to strengthen or weaken in several degrees over time according to activity levels. This makes up the needed adaptability for learning and memory. For example, neural circuits in the brain adjusted the strength of their connections in ways that correlated with changes in behavior and memory formation during such learning activities.

Further, derailments of normal synaptic functions have been connected to a wide array of neurologic diseases. For example, in Alzheimer's disease, there is a depot of beta-amyloid plaques disrupting synaptic function, which eventually causes memory loss and cognitive decline. This has been shown very clearly now by scientists, and it means to say that in Alzheimer's, the earliest stage—even earlier than any obvious problems in cognitive function—is that the synapses are malfunctioning. It simply underscores the great importance of synapse maintenance in maintaining cognitive functions.

2.2 Artificial Neural Networks

Artificial Neural Networks (ANNs) are a pivotal aspect of contemporary artificial intelligence, drawing inspiration from the biological neural networks that constitute human and animal brains. An ANN is structured as a series of layers containing interconnected nodes or "artificial neurons," each designed to mimic the function of biological neurons. These artificial neurons work together to process inputs, make calculations based on their programmed parameters, and generate outputs used for decision-making, pattern recognition, and predictions.

Structure and Functioning

The basic architecture of an ANN involves three types of layers: the input layer, hidden layers, and the output layer. The input layer receives raw data from the external environment, which is then processed in one or more hidden layers. Each hidden layer's neurons transform the inputs into something that the next layer can use. Finally, the output layer produces the final results or decisions based on the learned data features.

Each neuron in these layers is connected to several others in the next layer, and these connections, or edges, have weights that adjust as learning progresses. The process of learning in an ANN involves tuning these weights based on the errors in the output compared to the expected result. This tuning is often performed using a method called backpropagation, combined with an optimization technique such as gradient descent.

Basic Architecture of ANN:

To better understand the structure of ANNs, refer to the diagram below. It illustrates the input layer, hidden layers, and output layer, showing how data flows through the network.

Types of Artificial Neural Networks (ANNs)

Feedforward Neural Networks (FNNs)

Feedforward Neural Networks (FNNs) are fundamental structures in the realm of artificial intelligence. These networks are the simplest form of neural networks, where the information moves in one direction—from the input layer, through hidden layers, and to the output layer. The term "feedforward" indicates that there are no cycles or loops in the network.

FNNs can be visualized as a series of interconnected nodes, where each node represents an artificial neuron. The primary objective of these neurons is to receive input data, process it, and pass the processed data to the next layer. The structure of a typical FNN is as follows:

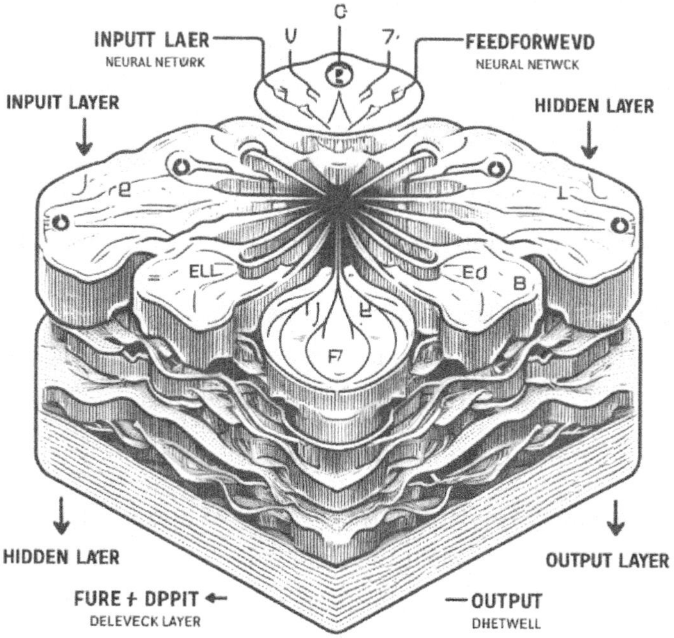

Figure 2.2: Feedforward Neural Network (FNN) Architecture

This figure depicts Feedforward Neural Network (FNN) architecture. FNNs are the most basic type of artificial neural network, and they serve as the foundation for many more complex neural network architectures. Information in FNNs flows in one direction only, from the input layer through any hidden layers, and finally to the output layer. There are no loops or cycles in the network, which is why they are called "feedforward."

The building blocks of an FNN are artificial neurons (represented by circles in Figure 2.2). Each neuron receives input from the previous layer (either the input layer or another hidden layer), applies a mathematical function (called an activation function) to process the data, and then sends its output to the next layer in the network. The connections between neurons are associated with weights (labeled "w" in Figure 2.2), which determine the strength of the signal between neurons. These weights are adjusted during the training process to improve the network's performance.

1. Input Layer: This layer consists of neurons that receive the raw data. Each neuron in this layer represents a feature of the input data.

2. Hidden Layers: These layers are where the actual computation happens. Each neuron in the hidden layer applies a weight to the input data and passes the result through an activation function to introduce non-linearity.

3. Output Layer: This layer provides the final output of the network. The number of neurons in the output layer corresponds to the number of classes in a classification problem or the number of predicted values in a regression problem.

Training an FNN involves adjusting the weights of the connections between neurons to minimize the error in the output. This process is typically done using backpropagation and gradient descent. During backpropagation, the error is calculated at the output layer and propagated back through the network, allowing the weights to be adjusted in such a way that the error is minimized.

Applications of FNNs:

- **Image Classification:** FNNs can be used to categorize images into different classes, such as distinguishing between different types of animals or identifying objects in a photo.

- **Spam Detection:** FNNs can filter out spam emails by analyzing the content and identifying patterns associated with spam.

- **Stock Market Prediction:** FNNs can be used to predict stock prices based on historical data, helping investors make informed decisions.

Recurrent Neural Networks (RNNs)

Recurrent Neural Networks (RNNs) are designed to handle sequential data, where the order of the data points is important. Unlike FNNs, RNNs have connections that loop back, allowing information to persist. This capability makes RNNs suitable for tasks where context and sequence matter, such as time-series forecasting, language modeling, and speech recognition.

The key feature of RNNs is their ability to maintain a memory of previous inputs through internal states. This is achieved by incorporating loops in the network, where the output from the previous step is fed back into the network along with the current input. The structure of an RNN is as follows:

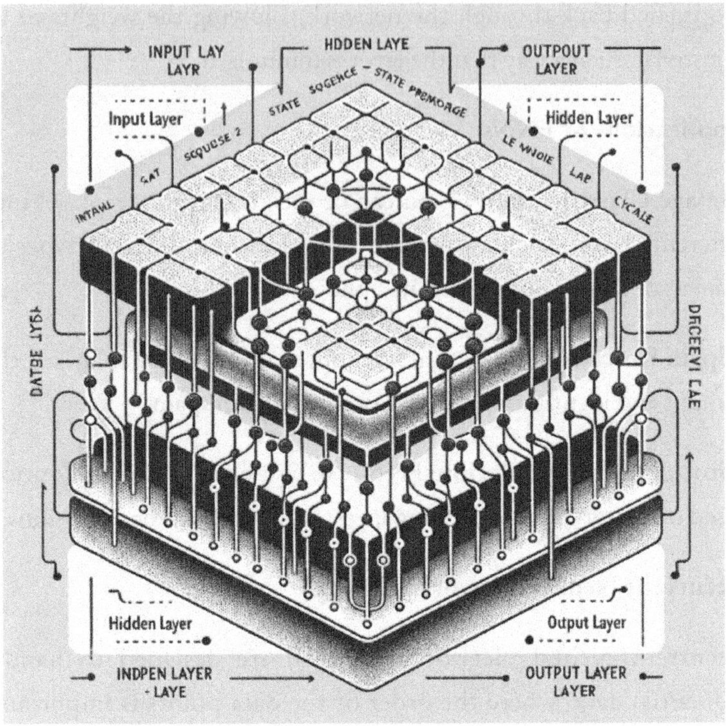

Figure 2.3: Neural Network (RNN) Architecture

This figure depicts a basic illustration of a Recurrent Neural Network (RNN) architecture. RNNs are a type of neural network specifically designed to handle sequential data, where the order of the data is important. Unlike traditional feedforward neural networks (FNNs), RNNs incorporate loops within their architecture, allowing information to persist across sequences. This enables them to perform tasks where context and history are crucial, such as time-series forecasting, language modeling, and speech recognition. The key element in an RNN that allows it to learn from previous data points is its internal state, often referred to as the hidden state (labeled "Hidden State" in Figure 2.3). At each time step, the RNN takes an input (labeled "X(t)" in the figure), along with the previous hidden state

(H(t-1)). These are then combined through an activation function to compute the current hidden state (H(t)) and the output (Y(t)) for that time step. The current hidden state captures the network's understanding of the sequence's history up to that point and is then fed back into the network along with the next input in the sequence.

1. Input Layer: This layer receives the sequential data.

2. Hidden Layers: These layers include loops that allow information to be passed from one step to the next, creating an internal state that captures the history of the inputs.

3. Output Layer: This layer produces the final output, which can be a sequence of values or a single value depending on the task.

Training RNNs involves a process called Backpropagation Through Time (BPTT), which extends the backpropagation algorithm to handle sequences of data. BPTT calculates the gradient of the error with respect to the weights by unrolling the network through time and then updating the weights accordingly.

Applications of RNNs:

• **Language Translation:** RNNs can translate text from one language to another by considering the context and order of the words.

• **Speech Recognition:** RNNs can convert spoken language into text by processing the sequential audio data.

• **Time-Series Prediction:** RNNs can predict future values in a time series, such as stock prices or weather data, based on past observations.

Convolutional Neural Networks (CNNs)

Convolutional Neural Networks (CNNs) are specifically designed to process data with a grid-like topology, such as images. They use convolutional layers to apply filters to the input data, extracting features such as edges, textures, and shapes. These features are then used for tasks like image recognition, object detection, and facial recognition.

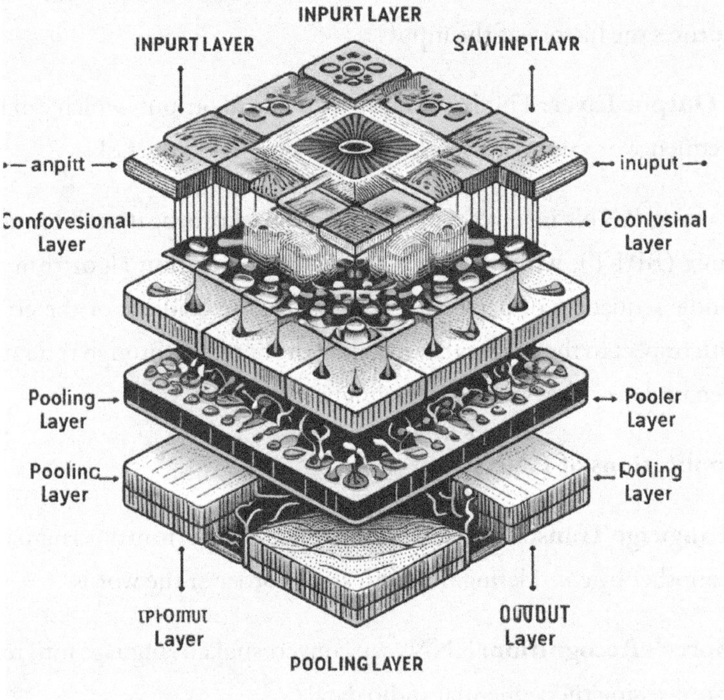

Figure 2.4: Convolutional Neural Networks (CNNs)

This figure depicts Convolutional Neural Network (CNN) architecture. CNNs are a type of deep neural network specifically designed to process data with a grid-like structure, such as images. They achieve this through the use of convolutional layers, which apply filters to the input data to extract features (as shown in the convolutional layers labeled "Conv Layer 1" and "Conv Layer 2" in Figure 2.4).

The structure of a CNN includes the following components:

1. Convolutional Layers: These layers apply convolutional filters to the input data to detect features. Each filter scans the input data and produces a feature map that highlights the presence of specific patterns.

2. Pooling Layers: These layers reduce the spatial dimensions of the feature maps, retaining the most important information while reducing computational complexity. Common pooling operations include max pooling and average pooling.

3. Fully Connected Layers: These layers perform the final classification or regression based on the features extracted by the convolutional layers. The output of the last pooling layer is flattened and passed to the fully connected layers.

CNNs are trained using backpropagation and gradient descent, similar to FNNs. However, the convolutional and pooling operations introduce additional challenges in terms of optimizing the network.

Applications of CNNs:

• **Image Recognition:** CNNs can identify and classify objects within images, such as recognizing animals in photos or detecting faces in security footage.

• **Medical Image Analysis:** CNNs can analyze medical images, such as X-rays and MRIs, to diagnose diseases and conditions.

• **Autonomous Vehicles:** CNNs are used in self-driving cars to recognize road signs, pedestrians, and other vehicles, enabling safe navigation.

Autoencoders

Autoencoders are a type of neural network used for unsupervised learning tasks, where the goal is to learn efficient representations of the input data. They consist of an encoder that compresses the input data into a lower-dimensional latent space and a decoder that reconstructs the original data from the latent space representation.

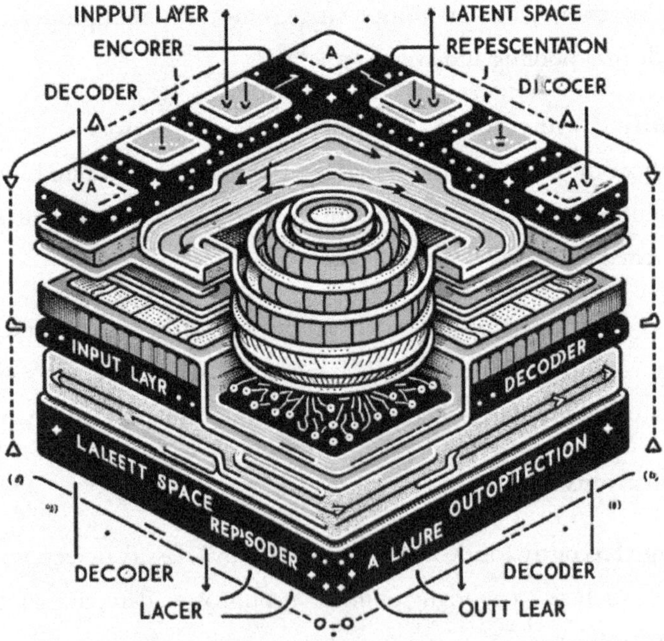

Figure 2.5: Autoencoder

This figure depicts a simplified illustration of an autoencoder, a type of neural network used for unsupervised learning tasks. Autoencoders aim to learn efficient representations of input data by compressing it into a lower-dimensional latent space and then reconstructing the original data from that compressed representation.

The structure of an Autoencoder includes:

1. Encoder: This part of the network compresses the input data into a latent space representation. It consists of multiple layers of neurons that progressively reduce the dimensionality of the data.

2. Latent Space Representation: This is the compressed version of the input data, capturing the most important features.

3. Decoder: This part of the network reconstructs the original data from the latent space representation. It consists of multiple layers of neurons that progressively increase the dimensionality of the data to match the original input.

Autoencoders are trained to minimize the difference between the original input and the reconstructed output. This is typically done using a loss function that measures the reconstruction error.

Applications of Autoencoders:

• **Dimensionality Reduction:** Autoencoders can reduce the number of features in a dataset while retaining important information, making it easier to visualize and analyze the data.

• **Anomaly Detection:** Autoencoders can detect anomalies in data by identifying deviations from the normal patterns learned during training. This is useful in applications such as fraud detection and fault detection in manufacturing.

• **Data Denoising:** Autoencoders can remove noise from data, making them useful in image and audio processing to enhance the quality of the data.

Generative Adversarial Networks (GANs)

Generative Adversarial Networks (GANs) consist of two neural networks, the generator and the discriminator, that compete against each other. The generator creates fake data from random noise, while the discriminator evaluates the synthetic data against real data and provides feedback to the generator. This adversarial process leads to the generation of new, synthetic data that closely resembles the real data.

This figure depicts a simplified illustration of a Generative Adversarial Network (GAN) system. A GAN consists of two neural networks, a generator (labeled "GENERATOR" on the left) and a discriminator (labeled "DISCRIMINATOR" on the right). The generator's role is to produce synthetic data (represented by the random noise "60°" feeding into the generator) that resembles real data. The discriminator's function is to analyze this synthetic data (labeled "20" and "400" on the left) and compare it with real data (labeled "ENTARI 250-400 AVERATA 0600" on the right). The discriminator's output (labeled "00" and "000") is a judgment on how well the generated data replicates real data. This feedback loop refines the generator's ability to produce ever-more realistic synthetic data.

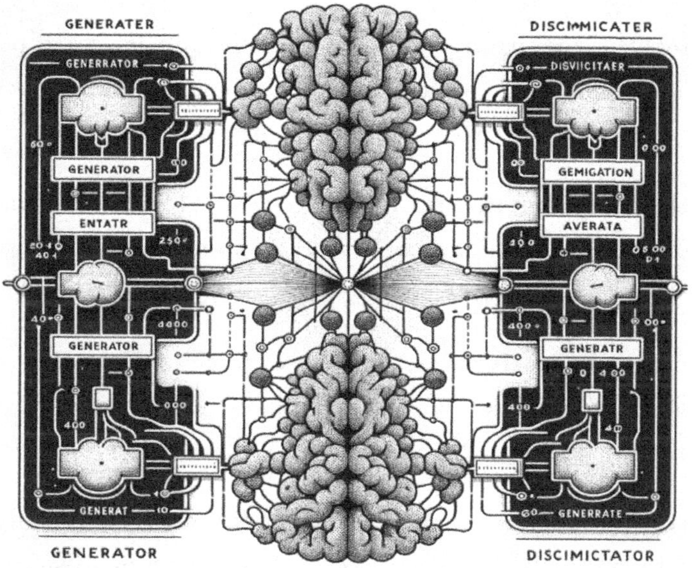

Figure 2.6: Generative Adversarial Network (GAN)

The structure of a GAN includes:

1. Generator: This network creates synthetic data from random noise. It consists of multiple layers of neurons that progressively transform the noise into a data sample.

2. Discriminator: This network evaluates the synthetic data against real data and provides feedback to the generator. It consists of multiple layers of neurons that classify the data as real or fake.

GANs are trained through a process of iterative optimization, where the generator and discriminator are updated alternately. The generator aims to produce data that is indistinguishable from real data, while the discriminator aims to correctly classify the data as real or fake.

Applications of GANs:

- **Image Generation:** GANs can create realistic images of people, animals, and objects, which can be used in applications such as video game design, virtual reality, and artistic creation.

- **Data Augmentation:** GANs can generate additional training data to improve the performance of machine learning models, especially in cases where real data is scarce.

- **Art and Creativity:** GANs are used to create new pieces of art, music, and other creative content, pushing the boundaries of what is possible in the creative industries.

Artificial Neural Networks (ANNs) are powerful tools in the field of artificial intelligence, capable of handling a wide range of tasks from image recognition to language translation. Different types of ANNs, such as Feedforward Neural Networks, Recurrent Neural Networks, Convolutional Neural Networks, Autoencoders, and Generative Adversarial Networks, are designed to address specific computational problems. By understanding the structure, functioning, and applications of these networks, we can better leverage their capabilities to solve complex real-world challenges.

2.3 Activation Functions

One of the most important building blocks of the Artificial Neural Networks (ANN) architecture is activation functions. In comparison with the biological neurons of the brain, these activation functions are very important in deciding whether a neuron should be activated by the received input or not. This is critically the form of decision-making in that it introduces the non-linear properties to the network, thus giving them the ability to learn and perform more complex tasks than networks made up of linear computation could do.

Purpose and Importance

The primary role of the activation function is to convert input signal of a node in an ANN to an output signal. That output signal now is used as an input for the next layer in the network. This is very key in allowing the learning of complex patterns in data. Activation functions introduce non-linearity, hence promoting the neural network to learn non-linear hypotheses. As a matter of fact, activation functions are very essential for neural networks in order to model complex relationships that exist between input and output variables, otherwise to be represented by simple linear predictions.

There are various types of activation functions.

1. Linear Activation Function: The linear activation function, also called the identity function, is one of the most basic activation functions used in neural networks. Mathematically, it's expressed as y = x, simply outputting the input value (x) directly. This function has a constant gradient (derivative) of 1, making it easy to train during the learning process. However, its inability to learn complex, non-linear relationships limits its applications in most hidden layers of neural networks. Therefore, other activation functions are more commonly used for these layers.

2. Non-linear Activation Function: Non-linear activation functions are crucial for introducing non-linearity into the neural network, allowing it to model complex data patterns. Common non-linear activation functions include sigmoid, tanh, and ReLU.

These functions enable the network to capture and learn intricate relationships within the data.

Sigmoid Activation Function: The sigmoid function, a popular non-linear activation function in neural networks, adds complexity crucial for real-world applications. Mathematically expressed as

y = 1 / (1 + exp(-x)),

it takes any real number as input (x) and transforms it to a value between 0 and 1 (y). Imagine an S-shaped curve! This characteristic allows the network to learn intricate patterns in data. While historically important, sigmoid functions can suffer from vanishing gradients in deep neural networks.

ReLU (Rectified Linear Unit): The ReLU (Rectified Linear Unit) activation function is a workhorse in deep learning, bringing non-linearity essential for complex tasks. Unlike the linear function (y = x), ReLU applies a threshold to the input. Mathematically, it's written as

y = max(0, x)

If the input (x) is positive, it remains unchanged (y = x). However, for negative inputs, the output becomes zero (y = 0). This creates a diagonal line where anything below zero is cut off. This simplicity makes ReLU computationally efficient and avoids the vanishing gradient problem that can plague other non-linear functions like sigmoid. These qualities make ReLU a popular choice for activation functions in many hidden layers of deep neural networks.

Tanh (Hyperbolic Tangent) Function: The tanh (hyperbolic tangent) function is another widely used non-linear activation function in neural networks. Mathematically, it's described as

y = (exp(x) - exp(-x)) / (exp(x) + exp(-x)).

Similar to sigmoid, it takes any real number as input (x). However, unlike sigmoid's 0 to 1 range, tanh squashes the input to a range between -1 and 1. Imagine a hyperbolic tangent curve stretched horizontally. This centered output makes tanh advantageous in certain scenarios. Additionally, tanh avoids the vanishing gradient problem that can hinder sigmoid function in deep networks. However, tanh can suffer from a phenomenon called "dead neurons" where some neurons become inactive during training. Overall, tanh offers a compelling alternative to sigmoid for introducing non-linearity in neural networks.

Leaky ReLU: The Leaky ReLU (Rectified Linear Unit) function addresses a shortcoming of the standard ReLU function. Mathematically, it's written as

y = max(α * x, x)

where α is a small positive value (typically 0.01).

For positive inputs (x), Leaky ReLU behaves just like ReLU (y = x). However, for negative inputs, it introduces a small, positive slope (y = α * x) instead of abruptly dropping to zero. This leak prevents the "dying ReLU" problem where neurons become permanently inactive during training. Leaky ReLU offers a good balance between the computational efficiency of ReLU and the ability to handle negative inputs, making it a popular choice for activation functions in deep neural networks.

Applications and Impact Activation functions are the functions that specify the output of the neural network model. Its choice sets how well the network models the data and generalizes to new, unseen datasets. For example, ReLUs are widely used within convolutional neural networks for tasks in image recognition simply because they enable the network to learn way faster with better performance. Further, the activation functions will define the ANN's solving ability, from simple binary classification tasks up to complex tasks; in these, the speech recognition and image processing are mentioned. The activation function one chooses directly impacts the performance of the neural network greatly. So, the selection of the activation function has to be, of course, very careful and upon the requirements of the application and, of course, on the specific characteristics of the data that is treated.

2.4 Learning in Neurons and AI

Learning is a fundamental feature shared by biological systems and artificial intelligence, enabling adaptation and the potential for excellence within varying environments. In biological systems, learning occurs at a neuronal level through a process referred to as synaptic plasticity. In artificial neural networks (ANNs), learning is achieved through training mechanisms like backpropagation, which modifies the weights and biases within the network.

Synaptic Plasticity in Biological Neurons

Synaptic Plasticity is the ability of synapses (the connections between neurons) to strengthen or weaken over time, in response to increases or decreases in their activity. This process is crucial for learning and memory formation in the brain.

Key Concepts of Synaptic Plasticity:

• **Long-Term Potentiation (LTP):**

LTP is the process of strengthening synapses based on recent patterns of activity. This occurs through high-frequency stimulation of the presynaptic neuron, leading to an increase in synaptic strength.

Learning to play a musical instrument involves repeated practice, which strengthens the synaptic connections between neurons involved in motor and auditory processing, leading to improved performance over time.

• **Long-Term Depression (LTD):**

LTD is the process of weakening synapses through low-frequency stimulation. This is essential for "forgetting" irrelevant information and allows the nervous system to remain adaptable.

Forgetting unnecessary details about a topic over time allows the brain to focus on more relevant and important information.

Importance of Synaptic Plasticity:

• **Adaptive Learning:** Synaptic plasticity allows the nervous system to adapt to new experiences and learn from them.

• **Memory Formation:** The strengthening and weakening of synapses are critical for forming and retaining memories.

• **Dynamic Adaptability:** LTP and LTD enable the nervous system to modulate synaptic strength in response to changes in activity and the environment.

Learning Through Backpropagation in Artificial Neural Networks

In artificial neural networks, learning is achieved through a process called backpropagation. Backpropagation systematically adjusts the connection weights between nodes in the network to minimize prediction errors.

Key Concepts of Backpropagation:

Training Step:

During training, the network makes predictions based on input data. The errors between the predictions and actual outputs are calculated.

Weight Adjustment: These errors are used to adjust the weights in the network to minimize the loss function using optimization techniques like gradient descent.

Iterative Learning: This process is repeated iteratively, allowing the network to learn and improve its accuracy over time.

Learning in ANNs:

1. Autonomous Driving Systems:

Convolutional neural networks (CNNs) are trained to process pixel data from images and recognize spatial hierarchies. These networks identify traffic signs, pedestrians, and other vehicles to make driving decisions.

Tesla's Autopilot system uses ANNs to process inputs from sensors around the car, learning to make real-time driving decisions.

2. Natural Language Processing (NLP):

Tools like OpenAI's GPT (Generative Pre-trained Transformer) learn from vast amounts of text data to make reasonable and sensible inferences or conclusions.

Intelligent bots can read and respond to customer requests effectively, enhancing customer service experiences.

Comparison of Biological and Artificial Learning:

Biological Learning:

• **Mechanism:** Synaptic plasticity (LTP and LTD).

• **Adaptation:** Strengthening or weakening synaptic connections based on activity.

Learning new skills or forming memories.

Artificial Learning:

• **Mechanism:** Backpropagation.

• **Adaptation:** Adjusting weights and biases in the network to minimize errors.

Training models to recognize patterns, make predictions, or generate text.

Learning in both biological neurons and artificial neural networks is a process of adaptation and optimization. Biological systems achieve this through synaptic plasticity, while artificial systems use backpropagation and optimization techniques. Understanding these processes helps in designing better AI systems and can provide insights into the functioning of the human brain.

2.5 Applications and Limitations of Artificial Neural Networks

Artificial neural networks have been the cornerstone of the incredible amount of applications of artificial intelligence, with their applications spreading over a variety of industries and disciplines. These systems are very good at operating in environments that require pattern recognition, classification, and prediction, leveraging their ability to learn from data in order to perform complex tasks. Despite their many advantages and successes, there are several limitations to ANNs that point to the challenges and areas for future improvement in the field of AI.

Large Amount of Applications

1. Speech Recognition: ANNs are fundamental to the development of speech recognition technology. Systems like Apple's Siri and Amazon's Alexa use deep learning models to understand and process human speech with remarkable accuracy. These systems continuously learn from new voice data, improving their ability to recognize different accents and dialects. Additionally, automatic speech recognition is used for tasks like voice search on smartphones, voice transcription services for meetings and lectures, and automated customer service systems.

2. Image Processing: In the realm of image processing, ANNs have been instrumental—especially convolutional neural networks (CNNs). They have been used in:

- Facial recognition systems for security applications, social media platforms, and personalized photo tagging;

- Medical imaging diagnostics to aid doctors in identifying tumors, detecting abnormalities in X-rays or MRIs, and even for early diabetic retinopathy detection from retinal images;

- Automated vehicles for real-time object detection and classification that enable features like self-driving car navigation and collision avoidance;

- Automated content moderation on social media platforms to automatically identify and flag inappropriate content based on image analysis;

- Anomaly detection in security systems to identify suspicious activities or objects in surveillance footage.

3. Financial Markets: In finance, ANNs are used to:

- Predict stock market trends and movements by analyzing vast amounts of historical and real-time data to forecast stock prices and assess risks;.

- Enable automated trading systems: that can react much faster than human traders, leveraging machine learning for investment decision-making.

- Detect fraudulent activities: by identifying patterns in financial transactions that deviate from normal behavior.

4. Medical Diagnostics: Deep learning models are increasingly being used in healthcare for:

• Disease diagnosis from medical imaging data: identify tumors from MRI scans or detect diabetic retinopathy from retinal images.

• Drug discovery: by analyzing vast datasets of molecular structures and biological information to speed up the development of new drugs.

• Personalized medicine: by tailoring treatment plans to individual patients according to their unique genetic makeup and medical history.

5. Natural Language Processing (NLP): ANNs are central to the NLP applications, such as:

• Machine translation: for real-time conversations, document translation, and multilingual content creation.

• Sentiment analysis: to understand the emotional tone of text in use in social media monitoring, customer reviews analysis, and market research.

• Chatbots: which can provide customer service, answer frequently asked questions, and even engage in conversation on various topics.

• Text summarization: to automatically condense lengthy articles or documents into shorter, key point summaries.

• Machine writing: to generate different creative text formats, such as poems, code, scripts, musical pieces, email, letters, and so forth.

3

Neural Networks and Brain Connectivity

We go into theintriguing field of brain connections and neural networks in this chapter.Consider the brain as a huge, networked network of neurons, each of whichinteracts with others to process information and respond. The basis of all wethink, remember, and do is this complex network. Comparably, neural networksserve as the foundation of contemporary artificial intelligence systems,allowing computers to learn, adapt, and make judgments.

With billions of neurons, each with a distinct purpose and function, make upneural networks in the brain. Synapses between these neurons enable electricalsignals to travel from one to the next. All that we accomplish, from basicreflexes to intricate problem-solving, depends on this mechanism. Gaininggunderstanding of these networks' workings helps us to create artificial neuralnetworks that resemble some of these features.

Though they are implemented with mathematical models and algorithms, artificialneural networks are modeled after the architecture of the brain. The artificialneurons, sometimes referred to as nodes, that make up these networks processand send data in layers. Specific tasks, such image recognition, languagecomprehension, and

even game play, can be trained into neural networks byvarying the connections and weights between these nodes.
Examining the interactions and cooperative function of various brain regions isthe study of brain connection. Scientists are better able to comprehend howdifferent brain regions distribute cognitive processes like memory andlearning. Similar ideas are put to use in artificial intelligence to createintricate neural network structures that can manage a wide range of difficultjobs.

3.1 Architecture of Neural Networks:

Artificial intelligence has been transformed by neural networks, which allow machines to undertake activities that were previously thought to be the exclusive purview of human intelligence. In this part, we will explore neural network architecture and design issues with an emphasis on their use in engineering applications like control systems, natural language processing (NLP), and image identification. We can value the strength and promise of these networks in many technical fields by knowing how they are built and operate.

The neural network's ability to handle complex tasks such as image recognition, natural language processing, and control systems is due to its layered structure and the use of activation functions like ReLU, sigmoid, and tanh. These functions introduce non-linearity, enabling the network to learn intricate patterns in data.

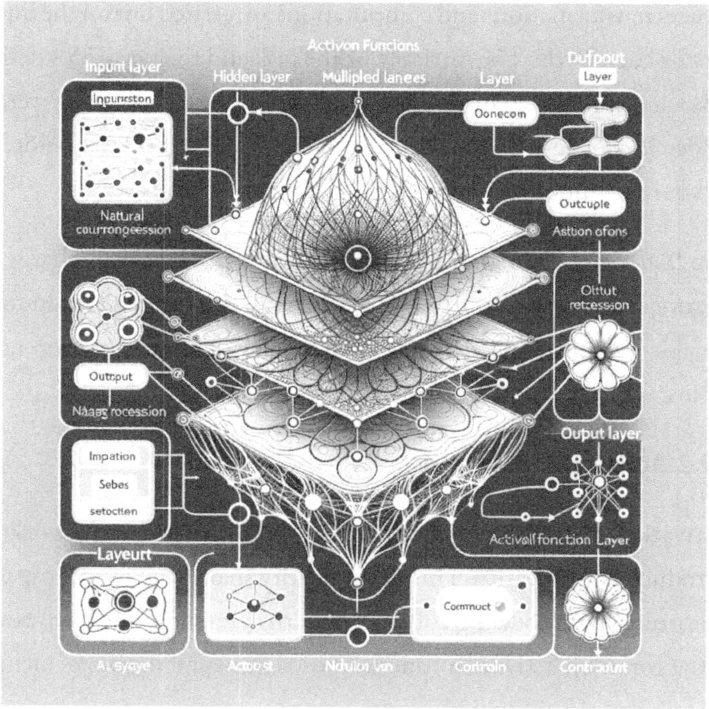

Figure 3.1: Architecture of a Neural Network

Three Basic Neural Network Components

Core to neural networksare interconnected layers of nodes, or neurons. The way these nodes function isintended to resemble that of real neurons in the human brain. Usually, a neuralnetwork has three kinds of layers:

The first level in a neural network, the input layer is in charge of gettingthe initial data. This layer's nodes each stand in for a feature or variablefrom the input data. Every node in image recognition, for instance, might standfor a pixel value from the image.

In between the input and output layers are the hidden layers.

Severaltransformations and computations are carried out on the input data by theselevels. The intricacy of the task and the network's design can determine howmany hidden layers and nodes are in each layer. A hidden layer's nodes arelinked to all of the nodes in the layer before it, and training modifies theweights of these connections.

The last level of a neural network, the output layer is in charge of creatingthe network's output. Every node in this layer stands in for a possible resultor forecast. Every node in an image classification task, for instance, canstand for a distinct class or category.

3.1.2 Activation Functions

Activation functions in neural networks allow the network to introduce non-linearity. This non-linearity makes the model capable of learning and modeling complex patterns present in the data. Some of the common activation functions used in neural networks include the following:

Sigmoid Activation Function: A sigmoid function helps to map an input value to an output in the range (0, 1). This is mainly useful in binary classification tasks. But, it has a vanishing gradient problem where gradients become very small during backpropagation, and its learning process becomes very slow.

Hyperbolic Tangent Function (Tanh): This activation function maps input values into an output in the range (-1, 1). This is similar to the sigmoid activation function, but this works better since it centers its output values around zero; it is very useful in the convergence stage of network training.

Rectified Linear Unit (ReLU) Activation Function: The ReLU function is defined as f(x)=max(0,x).

It has become the most widely used activation function in modern neural networks because of its simplicity and effectiveness. ReLU helps reduce the vanishing gradient problem. There is a big disadvantage with the ReLU function, however: the dying ReLU problem, in which the weights computed for a large number of negative inputs become zero and do not compute weights, making neurons dormant.

Leaky ReLU: Leaky ReLU is a variant of the ReLU activation function where the gradient is small and non-zero even when the input is negative. This helps handle the dying ReLU problem and can improve learning.

Softmax Activation Function: The softmax function is used in the output layer of classification neural networks. It converts the raw output scores into probabilities, facilitating multiple classes in classification.

3.1.3 Training Neural Networks

A neural network is trained by varying the weights of the connections between nodes to reduce the variance between the expected and real outputs. Usually, backpropagation is the algorithm used to carry out this procedure, which comprises the subsequent stages:

Forward propagation is computing the output by layer-by-layer passing the input data across the network.

Calculating the loss, or mistake, involves comparing the expected and actual outputs. Regression tasks' mean squared error (MSE) and classification tasks' cross-entropy loss are two examples of common loss functions.

The chain rule of calculus is used to calculate the gradients of the loss with regard to each weight in the backward propagation. These gradients suggest how to change the weights to lessen the loss.

Weight Update: Adam or stochastic gradient descent (SGD) is one of the optimization algorithms used to update the weights. Size of the weight updates is determined by the learning rate, a hyperparameter.

The network converges to a suitable degree of accuracy after several iterations, or epochs, of this process.

3.1.4 Image Recognition Architectures

Among neural networkapplications most well-known is image recognition. For this purpose, Convolutional Neural Networks (CNNs) are especially made, taking use of thespatial structure of images. Among the main elements of CNNs are

Convolutional Layers: These layers capture regional patterns like edges, textures, and forms by applying convolutional filters to the input image. Afeature map created by each filter emphasizes particular patterns in the picture.

Reducing the spatial dimensions of the feature maps, pooling layers preservethe most significant information while lowering computational complexity. Average and maximum pooling are common pooling operations.

Feature maps are flattened and run through fully connected layers following anumber of convolutional and pooling layers. To create the final result, suchclass probabilities, these layers merge the extracted features.

Dropout is a regularization method used to keep CNNs from overfitting. Duringtraining, every iteration a random subset of nodes is "dropped out,"or deactivated. The network is compelled as a result to learn strongercharacteristics.

3.1.5 Natural Language Processing Architectures

Work in naturallanguage processing (NLP) includes text production, sentiment analysis, andlanguage translation. Because recurrent neural networks (RNNs) can handlesequential data, they are often employed for these tasks, as are theirvariations, like Long Short-Term Memory (LSTM) networks and Gated RecurrentUnits (GRUs).

Recurrent Neural Networks (RNNs) are data processing systems that keep a hiddenstate that records data from earlier time steps. Each time step updates thishidden state according to the input at hand as well as the hidden state before it.

In networks with long short-term memory (LSTM): One kind of RNN created totackle the vanishing gradient problem is called an LSTM. They employ memorycells, specialized units that can hold information over lengthy durations. Bycontrolling the information flow, input, forget, and output gates found inLSTMs enable the network to learn long-term dependencies.

GRUs, or gated recurrent units, are a less complex and parameter-andgate-intensive version of LSTMs. They are more efficient computationally andalso tackle the vanishing gradient problem.

Attention Mechanisms: When predicting, attention mechanisms let the networkconcentrate on particular portions of the input sequence. When the network mustalign words in the source and destination languages, like in machinetranslation, this is especially helpful.

Transformers: A potent design for NLP problems, transformers process sequencesin parallel by purely depending on self-attention techniques. The foundation ofmodels like BERT and GPT, they have produced state-of-the-art outcomes in anumber of NLP benchmarks.

3.1.6 Architectures for Control Systems

Control systems involve tasks such as robotics, autonomous driving, and industrial automation. Neural networks used in control systems must handle real-time data and make decisions based on sensory inputs. Key architectures include:

1. Feedforward Neural Networks: Simple feedforward networks can be used for basic control tasks where the input-output mapping is straightforward. However, they lack the ability to handle sequential data.

2. Recurrent Neural Networks (RNNs): RNNs are well-suited for control tasks that involve sequential data, such as time series analysis and prediction. They can maintain a hidden state that captures the temporal dynamics of the system.

3. Reinforcement Learning (RL): RL involves training agents to make decisions by interacting with an environment. Neural networks, often called deep Q-networks (DQNs), are used to approximate the value function or policy in RL. These networks learn to maximize a reward signal by exploring and exploiting the environment.

4. Actor-Critic Methods: Actor-critic methods combine the advantages of value-based and policy-based RL approaches. The actor network learns the policy, while the critic network estimates the value function. This combination allows for more efficient learning and better performance in control tasks.

5. Model Predictive Control (MPC): MPC involves using a model of the system to predict future states and optimize control actions. Neural networks can be used to approximate the system dynamics, enabling efficient and robust control in complex environments.

3.1.7 Design Considerations

When designing neural networks for engineering tasks, several factors must be considered:

1. Data Quality and Quantity: The performance of neural networks heavily depends on the quality and quantity of the training data. Engineers must ensure that the data is representative of the real-world scenarios and sufficiently large to capture the underlying patterns.

2. Network Architecture: The choice of network architecture should align with the specific requirements of the task. For example, CNNs are ideal for image recognition, while RNNs and LSTMs are better suited for sequential data.

3. Hyperparameter Tuning: Hyperparameters, such as learning rate, batch size, and the number of layers and nodes, must be carefully tuned to achieve optimal performance. This often involves a process of trial and error, guided by domain knowledge and empirical results.

4. Computational Resources: Training deep neural networks can be computationally intensive. Engineers must consider the available computational resources, such as GPUs or TPUs, and optimize the network architecture accordingly.

5. Regularization Techniques: Regularization techniques, such as dropout, weight decay, and data augmentation, help prevent overfitting and improve the generalization of the network. These techniques should be incorporated into the training process to ensure robust performance.

6. Interpretability: Interpretability is crucial in many engineering applications, where understanding the decision-making process of the network is important. Techniques such as feature visualization, saliency maps, and model-agnostic methods can help improve interpretability.

7. Safety and Reliability: In safety-critical applications, such as autonomous driving and medical diagnosis, the reliability of neural networks is paramount. Engineers must implement rigorous testing, validation, and verification processes to ensure the safety and reliability of the network.

8. Ethical Considerations: Ethical considerations, such as bias, fairness, and privacy, must be addressed during the design and deployment of neural networks. Engineers should strive to create AI systems that are unbiased, transparent, and respectful of user privacy.

3.1.8 Applications of Neural Networks in Engineering

Neural networks have found widespread applications in various engineering domains. Here are some notable examples:

1. **Image Recognition**: Neural networks, particularly CNNs, are widely used in image recognition tasks. Applications include facial recognition, object detection, medical image analysis, and quality inspection in manufacturing.

2. **Natural Language Processing (NLP)**: Neural networks power many NLP applications, such as language translation, sentiment analysis, text summarization, and chatbots. These applications are used in customer service, content moderation, and information retrieval.

3. **Control Systems**: Neural networks are used in control systems for robotics, autonomous vehicles, and industrial automation. They enable real-time decision-making, adaptive control, and optimization of complex processes.

4. **Predictive Maintenance**: Neural networks can analyze sensor data from machinery and equipment to predict failures and schedule maintenance proactively. This helps reduce downtime and improve operational efficiency.

5. **Financial Modeling**: Neural networks are used in financial engineering for tasks such as stock price prediction, risk assessment, and algorithmic trading. They can analyze vast amounts of financial data and identify patterns that traditional models might miss.

6. **Healthcare**: Neural networks are transforming healthcare by enabling early diagnosis of diseases, personalized treatment plans, and drug discovery. Applications include analyzing medical images, predicting patient outcomes, and understanding genetic data.

7. Energy Management: Neural networks are used in energy management systems to optimize the generation, distribution, and consumption of energy. They help improve the efficiency of power grids, manage renewable energy sources, and reduce energy consumption in buildings.

8. Smart Cities: Neural networks contribute to the development of smart cities by enabling intelligent transportation systems, efficient waste management, and enhanced public safety. They analyze data from sensors and IoT devices to optimize city operations and improve the quality of life for residents.

The architecture of neural networks and their design considerations are critical for engineering applications. By understanding the components, training processes, and specific architectures for tasks such as image recognition, NLP, and control systems, engineers can harness the power of neural networks to solve complex problems and drive innovation. As the field continues to evolve, ongoing research and interdisciplinary collaboration will play a key role in shaping the future of neural networks and their applications in engineering.

3.2 Brain Connectivity

With billions of neurons assembling complex networks that allow us to think, feel, and act, the human brain is a wonder of sophisticated interconnectedness. In addition to giving us understanding of how our brains work, knowing the fundamentals of brain connectivity motivates creative engineering methods. Inspiring by the architecture and operation of the brain, this part investigates the engineering-related ideas of connection and network analysis. Graph theory and network resilience are important subjects, as are their uses in engineering problems.

Recognizing Brain Connectivity

Brain connection describes the interactions and communication between various brain regions. Within the brain, there exist three primary categories of connection:

Neurons are physically connected by structures called synapses and axons. Diffusion tensor imaging (DTI) is one method for mapping structural connectivity; it follows the diffusion of water molecules along white matter tracts.

The temporal association between the neural processes in various brain regions is known as functional connection. Real-time brain activity is recorded by methods like electroencephalography (EEG) and functional magnetic resonance imaging (fMRI).Effective connection is the causal influence that one brain system has over another. To offer a more thorough grasp of brain dynamics, it integrates anatomical and functional connectivity.

Through research of these kinds of connections, scientists can learn more about the cooperative interactions between several brain regions to carry out diverse cognitive tasks.

It is crucial for maintaining brain function despite disruptions. These concepts are also applicable in engineering for designing robust and efficient systems. Applications of hierarchical organization include image recognition, natural language processing, and other tasks that benefit from multi-level feature extraction.

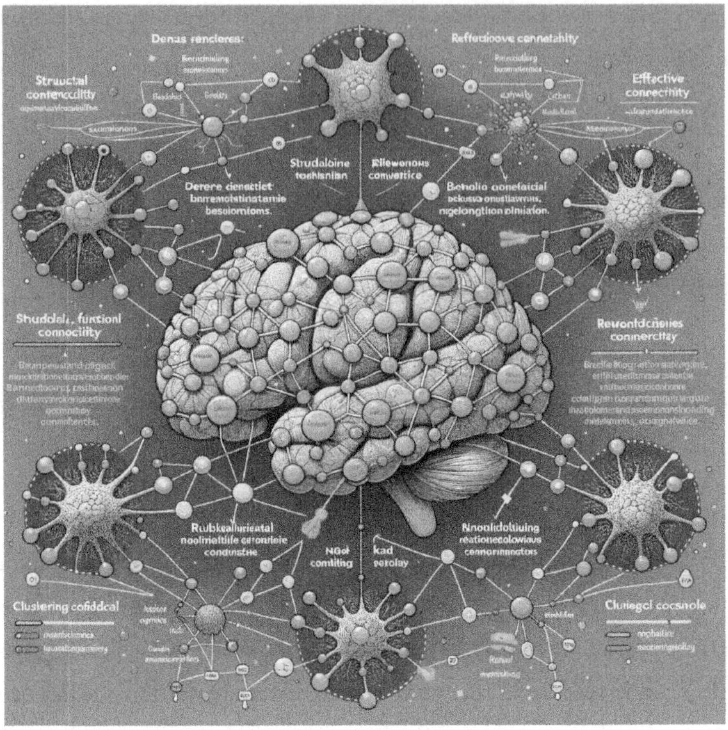

Figure 3.2: Brain Connectivity and Graph Theory Network resilience, which includes redundancy and robustness.

Industrial automation is another field in which neural networks find utility in controlling and monitoring intricate production procedures. Analysing sensor data, hierarchical networks can spot anomalies, forecast maintenance requirements, and streamline industrial processes. Through the capture of the hierarchical connections between various components and processes, these networks can enhance the dependability and efficiency of industrial systems.Furthermore, a method called transfer learning—in which a pre-trained model on one task is refined for another related task—is made easier by hierarchical structure in neural networks. Although the higher layers of the network are customized to the current activity, the lower layers, which record general features, can be reused. With relatively little data and computational resources needed for training, this method is very helpful for engineering applications with little data availability.Finally, a key component that makes neural networks capable of handling tasks requiring abstraction and feature hierarchy is their hierarchical structure. Deeply layered processing akin to that of the human brain allows neural networks to extract and integrate features at many levels, offering potent answers to challenging engineering challenges. Along with improving neural network accuracy and performance, this hierarchical technique opens up new engineering applications.

3.2.2 Brain Connectivity

Neurones or brain areas are represented by nodes, and the connections between them by edges, in the context of brain connectivity. The kind of the connections determines whether a graph is directed or undirected, weighted or unweighted.

Degree centrality counts the connections a node has. High degree centralitynodes are frequently essential hubs in brain networks that allow communication between many locations.

The amount to which a node is on the shortest routes between other nodes is known as betweenness centrality. High betweenness centrality nodes are essential to the effective network information flow.

The clustering coefficient quantifies the propensity of nodes to group together firmly. Regional processing depends on strongly connected brain areas, as seen by substantial clustering.

To what extent a network may be split into discrete modules or communities is known as modularity. Within the brain, modularity is linked to functional specialization, in which distinct modules carry out distinct functions.

The typical number of steps needed to travel across a network is known as the path length. Quick information processing in the brain depends on effective connection between nodes, which is shown by short path lengths.

3.2.3 Network Resilience

Resilience of a network is its capacity to continue operating in the presence of errors or interruptions. Brain resilience is essential to strong cognitive function and flexibility. Designing strong engineering systems can be informed by an understanding of network resilience.

Redundancy is the ability of information to flow between nodes via several routes. Redundancy in the brain makes sure that other pathways can be used to carry on communication in the event that one is interrupted. Redundancy can be included into engineering systems to improve fault tolerance and dependability.

The capacity of a network to survive attacks or outages is known as its robustness. Robustness in brain networks results from the existence of highly linked hubs that can make up for the loss of other nodes. In engineering, robust network design is locating and strengthening important connections and nodes.

Resilience to Unexpected Failures: Unexpected failures of nodes or edges happen. Because they are so highly connected and redundant, brain networks are typically resistant to random failures. Similar designs in engineering systems can help to guarantee continuous functioning even in the event of sporadic component failures.

Resilience to Targeted Attacks: The main goal of targeted attacks is to sabotage important links or nodes. Such assaults may be possible against brain networks if important hubs are taken over. Knowing this weakness can help engineers create dispersed critical function systems that lessen the effects of deliberate disruptions.

3.2.4 Applications of Connectivity Concepts in Engineering

Engineering applications of the ideas of brain connection and network analysis are many and range from creating reliable communication networks to transportation system optimization.

Communications Networks: Graph theory can be used by engineers to create robust and effective communication networks. Critical nodes can be found and routes optimized to improve the performance and dependability of these networks. Redundancy and modularity are two techniques that help to guarantee reliable communication even in the event of breakdowns.

Transportation Networks: Transportation networks can be treated with comparable ideas. Engineers can minimize traffic, optimize routes, and raise overall efficiency by examining the connectivity and flow inside these networks. Concepts of network resilience can be used to create transportation networks that can survive interruptions and continue to operate.

Reliability of the electricity supply depends critically on the stability of power systems. Power grid connectivity may be examined using graph theory, important components can be found, and systems that can bounce back from failures fast can be designed. Redundancy and robustness can help power systems be more resilient to both planned attacks and sporadic outages.

Neural prosthetics: Creating devices that can improve or restore neural functioning requires an understanding of brain interconnection. Engineers can create prosthesis that better interface with the brain by mapping the connection of brain regions engaged in particular functions, therefore enhancing the quality of life for those with neurological disabilities.

Healthcare Networks: Medical service delivery can be optimized in the healthcare industry by use of connectivity studies. Through knowledge of the connections between various healthcare institutions and providers, engineers may create systems that guarantee prompt and effective access to treatment. Furthermore useful in emergency preparedness and guaranteeing the strength of healthcare systems are network resilience principles.

Application of connectivity concepts can provide effective data flow and system resilience in the context of smart grids and the Internet of Things (IoT). Engineers can build strong, scalable, and able to manage the dynamic character of these networks systems by examining the connectivity of IoT devices and smart grid components.

Social Networks: Information on how information, influence, and behaviors propagate can be gained by examining the connectivity of social networks. Graph theory can be used by engineers to create algorithms that find communities, recognize powerful people, and maximise the sharing of knowledge. Furthermore contributing to the reduction of the effects of false information and strengthening of social media platforms is an understanding of network resilience.

Cybersecurity: By using network analysis, one can find weaknesses and improve the robustness of digital systems. Engineers may find weak places, provide redundancy, and create strong security measures to thwart cyberattacks by mapping computer network connectivity.

3.3 Parallel Processing

Intackling complicated and large-scale jobs, neural networks excel at parallelprocessing, which greatly improves their performance and efficiency. Inherentlypresent in the design of neural networks, parallel processing is the capacityto perform several computations at once. It is therefore very important todistributed systems and parallel computing in engineering.

In engineering, parallel processing is crucial for real-time applications like image recognition, natural language processing, and control systems. By distributing the computational load, neural networks can achieve faster processing times and improved performance.

Neural networks are by nature parallel structures. Numerous neurons that function independently of one another make up each layer of a neural network. A neural network processes an input simultaneously with all other neurons in the same layer as it is supplied into it. As data advances through successive levels, this simultaneous processing keeps going, enabling the network to manage enormous volumes of data fast and effectively.

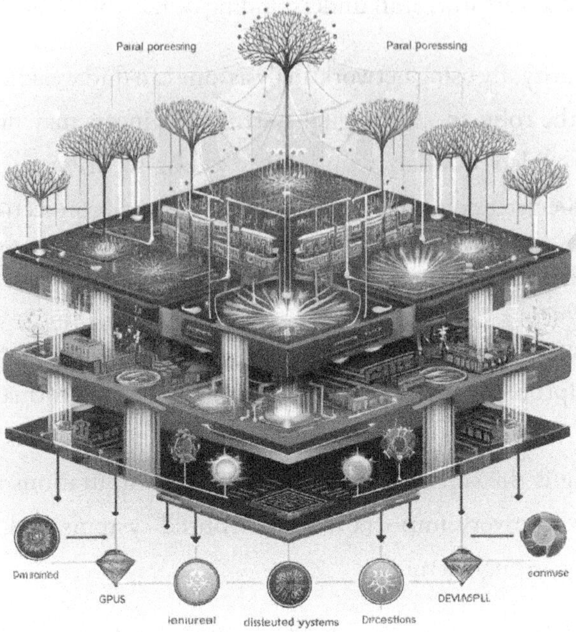

Figure 3.3: Parallel Processing in Neural Networks

Applications requiring high-dimensional data, such signal processing, natural language processing, and picture identification, benefit especially from parallel processing in neural networks. In image recognition tasks, for instance, every pixel can be processed concurrently, allowing the network to identify and analyze images remarkably quickly. In natural language processing, too, words or phrases inside a text can be analyzed simultaneously, enabling quick language translation, sentiment analysis, and other text-based applications.

The application of parallel processing in neural networks to distributed systems and parallel computing in engineering.

Combining several processors or computing nodes to carry out computations concurrently shortens the time needed to tackle difficult issues. Because of their parallel design, neural networks are ideal for use on parallel computing platforms including high-performance computing clusters, graphics processing units (GPUs), and multi-core processors.

Especially GPUs have been essential in enhancing neural network capabilities. GPUs are parallel processing specialized devices that can manage thousands of threads at once. They were originally created for graphic rendering. For big neural network training and operation, this makes them perfect. More accurate and sophisticated models can be developed by engineers using the parallel processing capability of GPUs to train neural networks quicker and on more datasets.

Distributed systems divide the computational load among several computers, therefore improving the parallel processing capabilities of neural networks even more. Smaller sub-networks that are processed on separate machines can be created from a big neural network in a distributed system. In addition to accelerating computation, this method enables the processing of enormous datasets that would be unfeasible on a single computer. Distributed systems frequently employ techniques like data and model parallelism to maximize neural network training and inference.

The process of data parallelism is dividing the dataset into smaller batches that are run concurrently on several computers. Every machine updates the model parameters according to the subset of data it processes and keeps a copy of the neural network. The finished model is formed by aggregating these modifications. Conversely, model parallelism is spreading the neural network itself over several computers. Parallel processing of several network components leads in the combination of the results to generate the final output. Both strategies improve neural network scalability and efficiency, which qualifies them for extensive engineering applications.

A key factor in neural networks' ability to manage complicated and large-scale tasks is their parallel processing capacity. Engineers may build more scalable and efficient neural networks by using the potential of distributed systems and parallel computing, which will stimulate creativity and tackle difficult issues in a variety of engineering domains.

3.4 Hierarchical Organization

One of the main characteristics of neural networks that allows them to manage tasks requiring abstraction and feature hierarchy is their hierarchical organization. This structure is modeled by the way that the human brain processes abstraction at various stages to enable the intricate interpretation and comprehension of sensory information.

Hierarchical structure in neural networks is accomplished by usage of several layers, each of which is in charge of extracting more abstract properties from the input data. The early, sometimes called lower, layers of a neural network are concerned with identifying basic forms, edges, and textures. These quite basic characteristics lay the groundwork for more intricate representations. Higher layers combine these basic characteristics as data moves through the network to create increasingly intricate patterns and things.

Convolutional neural networks (CNNs), which have extensive application in image identification and computer vision problems, are one example of this hierarchical technique. In a CNN, an image's first convolutional layer may identify edges; its second layer might combine these edges to identify shapes; and its third layer might identify things made up of those forms. High degrees of accuracy in tasks like object detection, face recognition, and scene understanding are made possible by this layered abstraction.

Beyond image recognition, the notion of hierarchical structure finds use in signal processing and natural language processing (NLP). Hierarchical models in natural language processing (NLP) include transformers and recurrent neural networks (RNNs), which at various levels capture the structure and meaning of language. Higher layers record phrases, sentences, and contextual connections between words; early levels may concentrate on identifying specific words and their elements of speech. This hierarchical knowledge allows NLP models to do remarkably accurate language translation, sentiment analysis, and text summarizing.

The hierarchical structure of neural networks is very helpful in engineering when addressing issues requiring various degrees of abstraction and feature hierarchy. Neural networks must, for example, interpret the context of the driving environment, evaluate raw sensor data, recognize things like cars and pedestrians, and make choices in real time. Effective handling of these many levels of abstraction by a hierarchical network design guarantees safe and dependable operation of the system.

Applications of hierarchical organization include image recognition, natural language processing, and other tasks that benefit from multi-level feature extraction.

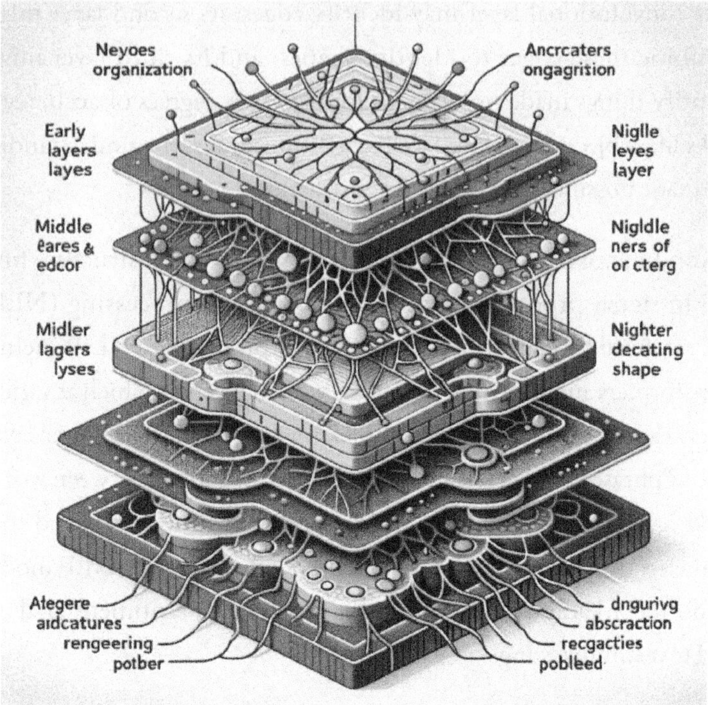

Figure 3.4: Hierarchical Organization in Neural Networks

Industrial automation is another field in which neural networks find utility in controlling and monitoring intricate production procedures. Analysing sensor data, hierarchical networks can spot anomalies, forecast maintenance requirements, and streamline industrial processes. Through the capture of the hierarchical connections between various components and processes, these networks can enhance the dependability and efficiency of industrial systems.

Furthermore, a method called transfer learning—in which a pre-trained model on one task is refined for another related task—is made easier by hierarchical structure in neural networks. Although the higher layers of the network are customized to the current activity, the lower layers, which record general features, can be reused. With relatively little data and computational resources needed for training, this method is very helpful for engineering applications with little data availability.

Finally, a key component that makes neural networks capable of handling tasks requiring abstraction and feature hierarchy is their hierarchical structure. Deeply layered processing akin to that of the human brain allows neural networks to extract and integrate features at many levels, offering potent answers to challenging engineering challenges. Along with improving neural network accuracy and performance, this hierarchical technique opens up new engineering applications.

3.5 Emergent Properties

In neural networks, emergent characteristics are sophisticated behaviors and capabilities that result from the interactions of network components that are simpler. The design, learning mechanisms, and data the network is exposed to cause these characteristics to arise; they are not specifically coded. Engineering systems must grasp these emerging characteristics since they can result in advances in self-organization, adaptive behavior, and general robustness of the system.

By Oneself

A fundamental emergent feature of neural networks is self-organization, in which the network independently creates representations and structured patterns from unstructured input data. In unsupervised learning, when neural networks—like autoencoders or self-organizing maps (SOMs)—learn to represent input in a compressed or clustered manner without labeled examples, this feature is very clear.

Autoencoders can be trained, for example, to compress images into lower-dimensional representations and then reconstruct them in image processing. By means of this procedure, the network learns the fundamental structure of the data, including common features or patterns, which it may thereafter apply to jobs like anomaly detection and image denoising. Engineering applications for self-organizing systems include resource allocation optimization, pattern detection in sensor data, and even sophisticated logistics network management without clear outside supervision.

Variable Behavior

In neural networks, adaptive behavior is the capacity of the network to adapt its responses to novel inputs or changing surroundings. Learning algorithms that change the weights and biases of the network to reduce error and enhance performance over time are what give it this flexibility. Reinforcement learning is a prime example of adaptive behavior, where neural networks learn to make decisions by interacting with an environment and receiving feedback in the form of rewards or penalties.

Development of intelligent control systems, autonomous robots, and dynamic resource management systems in engineering systems depends critically on adaptive behavior. To guarantee safe and effective navigation, neural networks, for instance, can adjust to changing road conditions, traffic patterns, and even unforeseen impediments in autonomous cars. Comparably, real-time optimization of production processes using adaptive control systems in industrial automation can react to variations in equipment performance or production demands.

Applications and Sturdiness

An other significant emergent characteristic is generalization, which is the ability of a neural network trained on one dataset to perform well on fresh, untested data. Engineering systems that must function dependably in a variety of uncertain settings depend on this feature. The design of the network, the caliber and variety of the training data, and the regularization methods applied during training to avoid overfitting all affect the capacity to generalize.

Generalization makes neural networks deployable in real-world situations with assurance that they will manage noise and variability well. For example, if the instances of new patients vary somewhat from the training data, a neural network trained on a wide dataset of medical images can generalize to identify them correctly. Ensuring the resilience and dependability of engineering systems in many applications and environments depends on this capacity.

Intelligent Emergence

Emergent intelligence, or the network displaying intelligent actions that were not specifically intended, is one of the most important consequences of emergent characteristics in neural networks. This covers being able to recognize intricate patterns, comprehend natural language, and even produce original material. Among neural networks exhibiting emergent intelligence are generative adversarial networks (GANs) and transformer models such as GPT-3.

Engineering can use emergent intelligence to create sophisticated AI systems that can handle jobs requiring a great deal of knowledge and inventiveness. AI-driven design systems can, for instance, produce creative product designs, maximize technical solutions, and even support scientific study by generating and verifying novel hypotheses. In engineering disciplines, these capabilities create new opportunities for efficiency and creativity.

Engineering Systems Implications

The design and use of technical systems are greatly impacted by the emergent characteristics of neural networks. Using self-organization, adaptive behavior, generalization, and emergent intelligence, engineers can create more flexible, efficient, and dynamically able systems.

Enhanced Automation: Emerging features make it possible to build very autonomous systems that can carry out intricate jobs with little human assistance. For sectors like manufacturing, transportation, and healthcare where automation may increase accuracy, productivity, and safety, this is especially helpful.

Enhanced Resilience: Emergent systems are frequently more resistant to disturbances and changes. While self-organization keeps them functional even in the face of partial failures or changing conditions, adaptive behavior enables them to react to unanticipated events.

Emergent intelligence in neural networks can stimulate innovation by revealing novel trends, coming up with original ideas, and streamlining intricate procedures. Innovations in materials research, pharmaceutical development, and environmental engineering might result from this capacity.

Scalability and Flexibility: Small-scale embedded systems to large-scale distributed networks can all benefit from the generalization and adaptability of neural networks. This versatility and scalability let engineers to use AI technologies in different industries and situations.

Responsible & Ethical AI: Handling ethical issues is another aspect of comprehending the emergent characteristics of neural networks. With an eye on problems like bias, openness, and accountability, engineers must make sure that AI systems are responsibly built and implemented. Through taking into account these elements, they can foster confidence and guarantee the moral application of AI technology.

Finally, the capabilities of engineering systems are advanced in large part by the emergent characteristics of neural networks. Engineers may create creative, robust, and effective solutions to difficult problems in many fields by leveraging self-organization, adaptive behavior, generalization, and emergent intelligence. These emerging characteristics of neural networks will propel additional developments and create new opportunities for engineering in the future.

4
Learning and Memory

Learning and memory formation are two integral building blocks of cognitive human functioning, no less in artificial intelligence. They are the processes by which novelty or information is acquired, stored, and used for solving problems. For the human brain, learning and memory occur through progressive biochemical processes, leading to the formation and strengthening of neural connections. Similarly, in artificial intelligence, these processes are implemented through algorithms that update the parameters of a neural network to optimize its performance.

Now consider a child learning to ride a bicycle. Certainly, the assuredness of controlling balance and coordination skills will not be there at the start. But the child can try repeatedly and learn to do better at each iteration. The child understands the errors being made at each trial and makes some corrections to later master the way of riding with confidence. In a very similar fashion, artificial neural networks learn from data. Repeated changes in parameter values, due to feedback, constitute the process by which a network becomes more capable of a task.

Learning in the human mind also operates on the principle of the varying strength of synapses, which through synaptic plasticity take place when an individual learns something new: the connections in neural circuits encoding this knowledge or skill are strengthened. In more general terms, synaptic plasticity allows the human brain to form new memories and retain learned knowledge. For example, in the event someone learns a new phone number, the connection between each of the neurons for each of the digits is strengthened, so it is easier for this person to recall that number later. Artificial neural networks practically do the same with these learning algorithms. The weight of the connection between artificial neurons is adjusted depending on input data and the desired output. One very popular learning algorithm is backpropagation, which keeps on updating the weight so as to decrease the discrepancy between predicted and actual values of output. The network learns from its mistakes and becomes more accurate as time goes on.

Most learning in biological and artificial learning systems can be grouped into types of learning. For instance, with the examples above, in the brain, learning includes both explicit learning—such as memorizing facts—and implicit learning, such as learning to ride a bicycle. It is the former but without applying consciousness to formulate how the motions are made. That said, artificial neural networks can learn by supervised learning, in which they are trained from labeled data, or unsupervised learning, in which they identify patterns in unlabeled data. Another class which is important in itself is reinforcement learning. This learning type arises from being conditioned through interaction with the environment, being rewarded for it, or being penalized.

Memory systems in the brain are equally complex. A good example is the short-term memory that allows us to keep a small amount of information for a short period of time, such as the use of a telephone number that can be dialed. On the contrary, long-term memory preserves massive information for a broad stretch of time so that we can refer to what happened earlier in life, knowledge, and skills. This distinguishes the storage mechanisms and the different architectures built in artificial intelligence.

Transfer learning is an important and interesting area in biological and artificial learning systems. People frequently transfer learned skills and knowledge to new contexts. For instance, having learned to play the piano, it becomes quite easier to learn any other musical instrument. Transfer learning in artificial intelligence is the technique of training a model on an initial task and then fine-tuning it for a distinct mission. Thus, it dramatically reduces the amount of data and resources in performed calculations during the training process and, therefore, it is invaluable for use in practical applications.

Forgetting and remembering are also important ingredients in learning and memory. The brain has facilities that involve pruning connections not necessary and strengthening those required by a certain task. The ability to forget task-irrelevant information allows for the emphasis to be on what is really important. In the artificial intelligence field, for example, regularization helps avoid overfitting by simplifying the model used and reducing reliance on specific details of the training data.

4.1 Mechanisms of Learning:

Learning and memory are central in both biological and artificial systems and underlie the processes of intelligence, adaptability, and problem-solving. In the brain, they are made possible by precise biochemical mechanisms and neural plasticity for enabling one to gain, store, and recall knowledge. In the AI field, it is done by algorithms that adjust parameters in neural networks to enable machines to learn from both data and experience. This section now turns to the mechanisms of learning in the brain and the relationship with machine learning algorithms used in engineering.

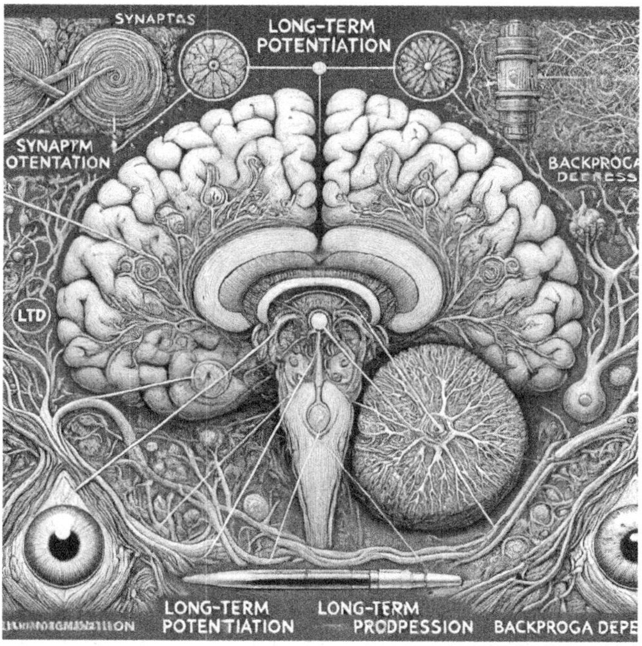

Figure 4.1: Mechanisms of Learning and Memory in the Brain

This diagram illustrates the mechanisms of learning and memory in the brain, highlighting synaptic connections, long-term potentiation (LTP), long-term depression (LTD), and the role of the hippocampus in memory consolidation. It also draws parallels to machine learning algorithms like neural networks and backpropagation.

• **Learning Mechanisms in the Brain**

Learning in the human brain is based on a complex process that takes place at the cellular and molecular levels. The basic units of the brain are the neurons, and they communicate with one another by using synapses. The phenomenon where all this becomes possible is called synaptic plasticity, allowing the synapses to either grow strong or weaken over time. This, at the underlying core, is the support that supervenes in learning and memory in the brain. There are several key mechanisms by which the brain learns:

Hebbian learning: The term is often heard in the phrase "cells that fire together wire together." It explains the phenomenon of the strengthening of synapses due to the concomitant activity of neurons. If two neurons are regularly active simultaneously, through a synapse, the very act between them gets strong, and as such, one will find it easy to activate the other in the future. The way associative learning can then be achieved is through the connections made between stimuli and responses.

Long-term potentiation is a durable increase in synaptic efficacy after high-frequency stimulation of the synapse. It is one of the main models of learning and memory mechanisms. LTP itself is brought about by the activation of NMDA receptors that produce an influx of calcium ions, thus triggering intracellular signaling pathways that strengthen the synaptic connection.

Long-Term Depression (LTD): In contrast to LTP, this is the process by which synaptic connections are actually weakened. It occurs as a result of relatively low synaptic activity, causing synaptic effectiveness to be reduced. LTD plays a very crucial role in synaptic plasticity, as it prunes away inappropriate connections and fine-tunes neural circuits.

The creation of such new neurons, or neurogenesis, occurs mainly in structures in the hippocampus, a part of the brain that enables learning and memory. These new neurons can incorporate themselves into the nature around them and, in so doing, promote plasticity and changeability of the brain.

Learning Processes: Synaptic Pruning As the brain matures and during adult life, synaptic pruning occurs where redundant synapses are eliminated and the remaining ones are reinforced. This effect enhances the efficiency of the neural circuits and is a process of fundamental importance for cognition and learning to develop completely.

- **Parallels in Machine Learning Algorithms**

Different machine learning algorithms that the way of operating can be compared with learning in brain power AI systems. Those algorithms tune parameters of the artificial neural networks for maximum performance on a task that it is designed to carry out. The most fundamental machine learning algorithms that draw an analogy with biological learning are as follows:

Supervised Learning: Supervised learning algorithms are technically related to the Hebbian learning of distributive information in a brain setting. Supervised learning is the kind of learning that involves training a neural network with data labeled by associating certain inputs with correct outputs. The learning algorithm modifies the synaptic strength between artificial neurons in the hope of minimizing the error between the output predicted by the network and the actual output. Techniques central to this learning include backpropagation, through which the error is propagated back in the network to change its weights.

Unsupervised Learning: Clustering and dimensionality reduction are unsupervised learning algorithms that take their motivation from brain ways to find out important patterns without explicit supervision. Such hidden structures are to be found within the data, which is, in most instances, unclustered.

Reinforcement Learning: Reinforcement learning can be thought of as a field closely associated with the physiological reward-based learning mechanisms of the brain. In reinforcement learning, we have a simple agent-environment framework rendering rewards or punishments to the agent based on its actions. And, the agent learns how to maximize its cumulative reward in AGI by changing its policy. This is just like the ways in which the brain learns by rewards or punishments its way of guiding future behavior.

Transfer learning can be described as a technique in learning where knowledge regarding a task is gained and put toward solving a correlated task. For example, it is just like a human does: using some previously learned knowledge to accomplish a newly arrived scenario. Most Simply, it is nothing but fine-tuning a pretrained model in a new data set, which drastically reduces the needs for data and time spent on training.

Regularization Techniques: A deep learning technique in regularization—say, dropout and weight decay—is that which eases overfitting by simplifying the model and lowering the dependence on finely set low-level parameters. Biologically, such regularization techniques are alike in the pruning of synapses, which makes neural circuits more efficient and general.

• **Learning and Memory Systems in the Brain**

Memory is a part of learning that enables an individual to retain and later retrieve information over some temporal extension. Human brain memory systems are very complex and include many regions and processes:

Short-Term Memory (STM) : Also referred to as working memory, the STM serves as a system of memory that is responsible for holding information briefly. Among the things it can do is hold a phone number just long enough for you to call it back. The working memory relies on the prefrontal cortex and other parts of the brain to hold on to information through the process of active rehearsal.

Long-Term Memory (LTM): A long-term memory stores information from a few hours to a lifetime. It is further divided into explicit (declarative) memory that demands conscious recall of facts and events and implicit (non-declarative) memory, which includes skills and habits. Memory traces laid down in the STM are stored in the LTM by a brain structure called the Hippocampus.

Memory Consolidation: This is the process by which STM is converted into LTM. This is completed by the stabilization of information and the integration of new memories into existing neural cell circuits. It is commonly thought that sleep, especially deep sleep, is essential for memory consolidation.

Retrieval and Reconsolidation: Retrieval is based on the procedure in which retrieved memories are recalled. Reconsolidation is said to occur at retrieval where it occurs as the modification and consolidation of retrieved memory. The entire procedure incorporates the dynamic ability of memories to change and get stronger over time.

- **Mechanisms on Memory in Machine Learning**

Machine learning mechanisms are also based on memory mechanisms to store all information that has been acquired. These include:

Training and validation: The machine learning model in the training stage learns from a given training dataset and tunes its parameters for minimizing the error function. The model's performance is thus validated during training using a distinct validation dataset to ensure generalization with respect to new data. It is similar to memory consolidation and retrieval by the brain.

Storage and Deployment of the Model: After training, machine learning models learned are stored for further use and then deployed to real-time tasks. In the same way that the brain retrieves stored memories for use, so, too, the machine learning model stores the learned information and recovers it for the inputs at hand.

Memory Networks: Memory networks are those belonging to Long Short-Term Memory (LSTM) and Gated Recurrent Units (GRU) networks, with inductive bias to handle sequential data and support long-term information preservation. The cells have memory to remember and update former information; this might contain the acquisition of longer-term dependency and the holding on to the context, analogous to how a human brain memory system operates.

Attention Mechanisms Attention mechanisms are now implemented in models like Transformers, due to which, the network is able to pay attention to parts of the input information relevant to the prediction. This mechanism provides better capability to process complex sequences and is inspired by how the human brain decides which input is important.

• Applications in Engineering

Further, understanding the mechanisms of learning and memory in both systems looks at engineering and the profound implications. It is parallel to these processes that have applications, hence it is why engineers develop AI systems that are more efficient and adaptive:

These learning algorithms range from navigation and manipulation to human-robot interaction, among many other fields. This allows a robot to learn from its environment and experience, changing or adapting its behavior with feedback so that the robot is more autonomous and flexible.

Healthcare: classified machine-learning models can be applied to the diagnosis of diseases, forecasting patient outcomes, and even personalized treatment. Thanks to memorization, the models can harness the historical data of all patients and give accurate and timely insight.

Finance In finance, machine learning algorithms mimic the recommended portfolio theory using great datasets that would create a trend to follow in prediction movements in specific markets. Transfer learning and attention make the model even stronger in adapting to tvá creeks markets and providing reliable predictions of a specific security.

NLP applications, including language translation, sentiment analysis, and text summarization, rely on models that require the ability to understand and express human language. The memory network and attention mechanism enhance the ability of the model to capture context and generate coherent responses.

Autonomous Vehicles: Machine learning drives autonomous vehicles. It enables building the environment perception, making decisions, and safely navigating. The merge of learning and memory mechanisms, due to which this system may show adaptability to different driving conditions, enables improvements in time .

- **Ethical Considerations**

Hence, in the process of developing advanced AI models that emulate such a learning and memory mechanism within the human brain, questions about the ethical implications should not be ignored. Issues such as fairness, transparency, and accountability have been squarely brought into the public limelight. Some ethical considerations are as follows:

Bias and Fairness: Machine learning models have to be trained on all different, representative datasets in order to avoid causing bias, whose results can be unfair or even discriminatory. These findings emphasize that unbiased AI systems are an important factor in allowing the general acceptance of using AI models.

Transparency: Trust is gained when one knows how artificial intelligence systems reach decisions. The enhanced understanding brought by the transparent models and explanations of functioning have the characteristic of inciting trust by the user in the systems.

Privacy: AI applications should safeguard user data and privacy. Responsible AI must ensure stringent data security and privacy in compliance with all regulations. Accountability: Administrative accountability in AI systems has to be designed clearly with any possible negative outcomes in mind. Developers, users, and policymakers need to collaborate in the design of the guidelines and regulations that define the responsible implementation of AI technologies.

Understanding the mechanisms of learning and memory in the brain provides valuable insights in the development of improved machine learning techniques. Bridging this gap between biological and artificial systems will help enable AI technologies and systems in general to be developed with high efficiency, adaptation, and flexibility in dealing with various engineering problems. Knowing processes like these also open ways to ethical matters of AI development, making sure such strong technologies are responsibly used for the well-being of mankind.

4.2 Learning Algorithms:

Machine learning refers to algorithms that make artificial intelligence systems learn from input data, discover patterns, and improve with use. This set of algorithms comprises a block that handles supervised learning, unsupervised learning, and reinforcement learning, and is widely used in most methodologies related to the engineering field. The following section presents how these machine learning algorithms work in fine detail and the applications of engineering behind these methodologies.

Figure 4.2: Various Machine Learning Algorithms

This comprehensive diagram shows various machine learning algorithms, including supervised learning (linear regression, decision trees), unsupervised learning (clustering, PCA), and reinforcement learning. It also highlights their applications in engineering, such as image recognition, natural language processing, robotics, and predictive maintenance.

Supervised Learning

Supervised learning is that part of machine learning where the model learns from labeled data. In supervised learning, there is an output for each training example that indicates the right answer or label.

Supervised learning basically tries to learn a mapping from inputs to outputs which would generalize to new, unseen data.

1. Principles and Techniques: Principles and Techniques Of course, there is a training phase in the case of supervised-learning-related algorithms where the labeled data are utilized and then a testing phase where the model is put to the test on a new set of data. The following techniques are the most common:

• Linear Regression: Used for continuous-valued outputs; in other words, it models considered the relationship between input features and a continuous output by fitting a linear equation to the data. Such models find widespread use in forecasting and trend analysis in domains like economics and engineering.

• Logistic Regression: This term is used when binary classification is needed. As in the case of medical diagnosis, logistic regression determines the probability of a given input being a member of a given class. Another related example is spam detection.

• Support Vector Machines (SVMs): SVMs are among the popularly used algorithms to solve both classification and regression problems. They find a hyperplane that separates the feature space best to demarcate classes. Applications of SVMs are in high-dimensional spaces and in image recognition and bioinformatics.

• Decision Trees: These are models that make decisions based on input features through a tree-like structure. These are interpretable and hence can handle both categorical and continuous data, hence are used in varied fields like finance and healthcare.

• Random Forests: An ensemble method applying plural decision trees to deliver higher accuracy and robustness. Random forests find application in credit scoring and fraud detection.

• Neural Networks: These are interconnected nodes that are arranged in multiple layers, just like in the case of a human brain. Neural networks are very effective in working with complex problems, such as image and speech recognition. Deep learning is a subset of neural networks, wherein we keep stacking layers to find very fine, complex patterns in the data.

2. Engineering Applications: Supervised learning algorithms find a lot of engineering applications out of the following:

• Image recognition: Examples of using CNNs for image recognition include object detection, facial recognition, and medical image analysis. For autonomous driving, it aids in recognizing pedestrians, traffic signs, and other cars.

• Natural language processing: RNNs and transformers form the backbone of translation, sentiment analysis, and text generation. Example aspects include customer service where used models generate understanding and generation responses to users in chatbots.

• Predictive maintenance: Supervised learning models are used in the prediction of equipment failure and time scheduling of maintenance for triggered efficiency, especially in manufacturing and industrial processes. Other areas are financial forecasting: prediction of stock prices, market states, and economic indicators to guide the actions of financial institutions.

• Medical Diagnosis: Supervised learning algorithms could be applied to medical data to diagnose diseases, predict patient outcomes, and provide personalized care, to improve the life of these patients.

Unsupervised Learning

Here the model is trained with data points or patterns but with no explicit supervision signal or designated examples. Unsupervised learning is useful for clustering, dimensionality reduction, and outlier detection.

1. Principles and Methods: Unlike supervised learning, algorithms in unsupervised learning do not operate with the labels of output but with the structure of the data. Some of the common techniques of unsupervised learning are:

2. Clustering: These are algorithms that group similar data points together. Some common methods of clustering include:

• K-Means Clustering: This algorithm partitions the data into some K groups such that each member belongs to the group with the nearest mean. This K-Means algorithm is largely used in market segmentation, image compression, and document clustering.

• Hierarchical Clustering: This creates a dendrogram of hierarchically organized clusters, either from an agglomerative approach—combining items from the bottom—or based on divisions from the top. Bioinformatics applications of such methods involve gene expression analysis, while social network analysis is another example.

• DBSCAN (Density-Based Spatial Clustering of Applications with Noise): It detects clusters based on the density of data points and therefore locates clusters of arbitrary shape while detecting noise. DBSCAN can be easily extended for geographic information systems as well as for anomaly detections.

2. Dimensionality Reduction: These are the techniques of reducing the number of features in your data. Some techniques are:

• PCA: Basically changes the data into a lower-dimensional space by detecting principal components that are very useful in catching variance. One may use PCA for data visualization, noise reduction, and feature extraction.

• t-Distributed Stochastic Neighbor Embedding (t-SNE): This is a complex nonlinear dimensionality reduction technique that is very helpful for high-dimensional data visualization. The most common applications are detected in bioinformatic studies and text mining.

• Autoencoders: Neural network architectures meant to learn a compact representation of the data. These consist of an encoding step, during which the data is subject to a kind of compression, and a decoding step, when the data is reconstructed. Autoencoders are normally used for data recovery, anomaly detection, and dimension reduction.

3. Anomaly Detection: The definition of an observation that is an outlier to the baseline or unusual relative to the rest. Some common techniques include:

• Isolation Forest: An isolation forest is an ensemble method to isolate anomalies by randomly partitioning the data. A good example of such a forest is in fraud detection, network security, and fault detection.

• One-Class SVM: It is employed in such a way that the model trains to recognize normal data and is strange when anomalous data are a departure from what the model has learned. An example of such usage includes intrusion detection and quality control.

4. **Engineering Applications:** In fact, unsupervised learning applications in engineering are vast and varied:

• Customer Segmentation: Clustering algorithms group customers based on common purchasing behavior, demographics, and preferences, enabling businesses to offer a more personalized marketing strategy and foster increased customer satisfaction.

• Anomaly Detection: For instance, the reliance on the unsupervised learning algorithm by industrial systems can be massive in detecting any abnormal behaviors or anomalies that could be in the data; for example, fraud detection, network security, fault detection, among others.

• Data preprocessing is done for techniques such as PCA and autoencoders so that the complexity of data can be properly reduced, in turn improving the performance of machine learning models in tasks like image recognition and NLP.

• Recommendation Systems: The group of different types of similar items or users is done by clustering algorithms, and recommendation systems use these groups to suggest related products, movies, or content based on user interests and behaviors.

• Bioinformatics: Unsupervised learning analyzations of genetic data for discovering patterns, clustering genes with similar expression profiles, and coming up with insights on biological occurrences or disease aspects from the data set.

Reinforcement learning

Essentially, this is a type of machine learning where an agent learns so that it quickly lands on the policy via an interaction with the environment and feedback that would be presented in the form of rewards and penalties whose eventual outcome will have to be the maximization of long-term reward.

1. Principles and Techniques: Reinforcement learning can require a number of general components from an agent, environment, states, actions, and rewards Mechanisms/ Techniques in RL;

i. Value-Based: These are the kinds of mechanism that quantifies the function of values for an expected cumulative award condition per state-action pair. Techniques include:

• Q-Learning: An off-policy algorithm that learns the value of taking a particular action in a given state. It will update the Q-values based on the reward received and the maximum Q-value of the next state.

• SARSA (State-Action-Reward-State-Action): It will update the Q-values based on the action actually taken in the next state. SARSA is more conservative than Q-Learning, used in those applications where exploration is very important.

ii. Policy-Based Methods: Policy-based methods optimize parametrized policies with respect to the expected return. Examples are:

• REINFORCE: A policy-gradient method for optimizing stochastic policies; the final objective function is obtained using the likelihood ratio. Generally, for tasks with continuous action spaces, e.g., robotic control.

• Actor-critic methods: A value-based and a policy-based method together. The actor learns the policy, and the critic is responsible for the estimation of the value function. This combination improves stability and convergence in RL.

iii. Model-based methods: Involves learning a model of the environment. Techniques comprise learning and using a model of the environment to simulate and plan actions. Some of the most popular techniques include:

• Dyna-Q: This approach combines Q-Learning and a model-based approach. The agent learns a model of the environment and uses it for generating additional training experiences, thereby increasing learning.

• Monte Carlo Tree Search (MCTS): A planning algorithm for the creation of a search tree based on action simulations and the consequential decision at each step. MCTS is widely used in game playing and autonomous systems.

2. Engineering Applications: The reinforcement learning technique is used in many engineering applications. Among them are:

• Robotics: RL algorithms help robots learn complicated tasks like object grasping, environment navigation, and interaction with humans. Robots can adapt and learn from the feedback they receive for their actions, hence improving their performance over time.

• Energy Management: Applying RL to training in the domain of self-driven vehicles for navigation in complex traffic scenarios, making decisions, and optimizing the route according to an objective function. The agent learns to interact with the environment, trying to maximize the rewards and ensuring safety and efficiency.

• Energy Management: A lot is achieved by applying RL in energy management, buildings, smart grids, and industrial processes, as the system learns through historical data and environmental conditions in the reduction of costs and promoting sustenance.

• Finance: It finds application in portfolio management, algorithmic trading, and risk management. With the ability to learn from market data and feedback, such models make intelligent decisions in order to maximize profits and minimize risks.

• Healthcare: Personalized treatment planning, medical interventions, and drug discovery. Simulating responses from the patient and feedback from clinical outcomes make for better delivery of health care and patient outcomes.

• Industrial Automation: The RL algorithms are applied in the manufacturing process in the aspects of process optimization, supply chain management, and predictive maintenance. These systems learn from their experience through sensors that reveal data or direct operational feedback. The concept Other Concepts Comparative analysis and integration

Comparison and Integration

While supervised, unsupervised, and reinforcement learning each has independent methodologies and applications, they can also be integrated in ways that bring them together more cohesively and flexibly in creating AI systems. Semi-supervised learning, for example, marries labeled data with unlabeled data to enhance model performance, while transfer learning draws mostly on pre-trained models originating from supervised learning to enhance RL or unsupervised models.

i. Semi supervised learning is a type of learning in which both labeled and unlabeled data are used for learning, based on the notion that many classes can be learned from relatively few labels. It is especially useful when labeled data is costly or time-consuming to obtain. Techniques in this approach are self-training, co-training, and multi-view learning. Applications include image classification, text classification, and speech recognition.

ii. Transfer learning is the application of a model pre-trained on one task, which then has fine-tuning for any related task undertaken. This significantly cuts down the time it takes to train and amounts of data that are required. Transfer learning is primarily used in the fields of image recognition, natural language processing, and domain adaptation.

iii. Multi-agent reinforcement learning—Multiple agents share their environment, learning from it—this is used in many applications, from collaborative robotics to autonomous driving and game playing. Individual learning—Within independent agents—cooperative learning—competitive learning—.

iv. Self-Supervised Learning Self-supervised learning, on the other hand, is where supervisory signals are created from the data unlabeled, which, in turn, enables learning in models from the created representations. The major subfields include contrastive learning, predictive coding, and masked language models. Some of the applications are in computer vision, natural language processing, and speech processing.

• Ethical Issues

As with any AI technology, there would be ethical issues in the development and deployment of machine learning algorithms. The emphasis will be on fairness, transparency, responsibility, and privacy to ensure the responsible development of AI.

• Fairness: Machine learning models need to be trained on diversified and representative datasets to avoid bias and prevent the risk of resulting in unfair or discriminatory outcomes. Fairness is key to trusted systems across the board in the use of AI.

• Transparency: There should be the understanding of the mechanics all behind the decisions that AI does, apart from or results in, to inject trust. Transparent models and the processes by which decisions are made should be evident in their explanation.

• Security: The security and privacy of user data must be guaranteed at all costs by AI applications. This will include strong data protection measures and conformation to privacy regulations that may relate to imposed regulations.

• Accountability: Make clear lines of responsibility by AI systems to deal with the possible harms or misuses. That requires developers, users, and policy-makers to work toward creating rules and regulations that will lead to this assured liability in the deployment of AI technologies.

The learning algorithms of supervised, unsupervised, and reinforcement bring a very different kind of capability and application into engineering. Such knowledge would help an engineer develop AI systems that are more effective, adaptive, and can handle significant complexity in problem-solving processes. Integration among these learning strategies and reflecting on the ethical values will serve to bulldoze more strongly the impacts and acceptance of AI technologies across several fields.

4.3 Memory Systems:

Memory systems are fundamental to both biological and artificial systems, playing a crucial role in how information is stored, retrieved, and utilized. In the brain, memory is a complex process involving various regions and mechanisms that allow us to retain and recall information. Similarly, engineering systems employ different types of memory to manage and process data efficiently. This section explores the memory systems in the brain and their analogs in engineering, such as caching mechanisms in computer architecture and database systems.

This detailed diagram compares memory systems in the brain and their analogs in engineering systems. It highlights brain regions involved in memory (e.g., hippocampus, prefrontal cortex) alongside computer architecture components like caches and databases. It shows the parallel between short-term and long-term memory in biological and artificial systems.

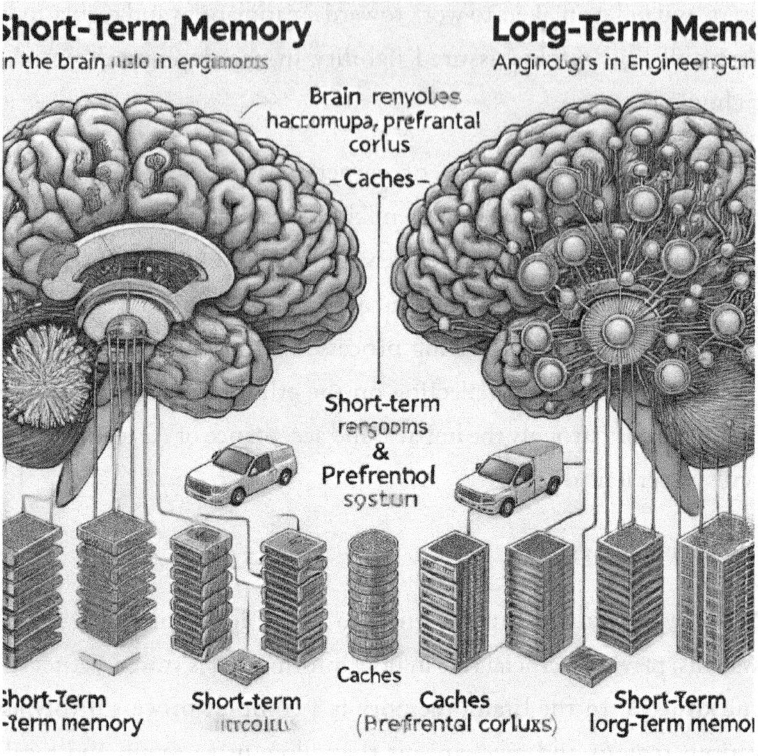

Figure 4.3: Memory Systems in the Brain and Engineering Systems

• Memory Systems in the Brain

The human brain's memory system is incredibly intricate, involving multiple regions and processes to store, retrieve, and manipulate information. Memory can be broadly categorized into short-term and long-term memory.

Short-Term Memory (STM), also known as working memory, allows us to hold a small amount of information temporarily. This type of memory is essential for daily tasks, such as remembering a phone number long enough to dial it or holding a conversation. STM relies heavily on the prefrontal cortex and other associated regions that help maintain and manipulate information for short periods.

In contrast, Long-Term Memory (LTM) stores information for extended periods, ranging from hours to a lifetime. LTM can be further divided into explicit (declarative) memory and implicit (non-declarative) memory. Explicit memory involves conscious recall of facts and events, which can be episodic (personal experiences) or semantic (general knowledge). The hippocampus plays a critical role in consolidating these memories, transferring information from short-term to long-term storage.

Implicit memory includes skills and habits that we perform automatically, such as riding a bicycle or typing on a keyboard. This type of memory is stored in various brain regions, including the basal ganglia and cerebellum, which are involved in motor control and coordination.

Memory consolidation is a vital process where short-term memories are transformed into long-term memories. This involves the stabilization and integration of new information into existing neural networks. Sleep, particularly deep sleep, enhances memory consolidation by promoting synaptic plasticity and the reorganization of neural circuits.

Retrieval and reconsolidation are processes where stored memories are accessed and potentially modified. Retrieval involves recalling stored information, while reconsolidation allows for the reinforcement and updating of memories upon retrieval. This dynamic process ensures that memories remain relevant and adaptable to new information.

Memory Systems in Engineering

In engineering, memory systems are designed to manage and process data efficiently, drawing inspiration from biological memory mechanisms. Key analogs include caching mechanisms in computer architecture and database systems.

Caching Mechanisms in Computer Architecture:

Caching is a crucial concept in computer systems, where it serves as a high-speed storage layer that temporarily holds frequently accessed data. The primary goal of caching is to reduce the time it takes to access data from the main memory or disk storage. This process mirrors the brain's use of short-term memory to store and quickly retrieve relevant information.

Caches are typically implemented at multiple levels in computer architecture:

- L1, L2, and L3 Caches: Modern processors include multiple levels of cache, each with different speeds and sizes. L1 cache is the smallest and fastest, located closest to the CPU core. L2 and L3 caches are progressively larger and slower but still much faster than accessing data from the main memory. This hierarchical structure ensures that the most frequently used data is readily available, similar to how short-term memory works in the brain.

- Cache Coherency: In multi-core processors, cache coherency ensures that all cores have a consistent view of the data. This involves protocols that manage the synchronization of data across multiple caches, preventing inconsistencies and ensuring efficient parallel processing.

Database Systems and Caching:

In database systems, caching mechanisms are employed to enhance performance and reduce latency in data retrieval:

• Database Caches: These caches store frequently accessed data and query results, reducing the need to repeatedly fetch data from the underlying storage. This approach speeds up database operations, much like how the brain quickly retrieves information from short-term memory.

• In-Memory Databases: Some databases store entire datasets in memory, allowing for extremely fast access and manipulation of data. This is analogous to the brain's use of working memory to hold and process information in real-time.

• Indexing and Query Optimization: Databases use indexing and query optimization techniques to improve data retrieval efficiency. Indexes act like memory cues in the brain, providing quick access paths to the required data. Query optimization ensures that data retrieval operations are performed in the most efficient manner, similar to how the brain optimizes the recall process.

Long-Term Storage and Memory Management:

Engineering systems also incorporate long-term storage solutions to manage large volumes of data over extended periods:

• Hard Disk Drives (HDDs) and Solid-State Drives (SSDs): These storage devices provide long-term data storage, analogous to the brain's long-term memory. HDDs offer larger storage capacities at lower costs, while SSDs provide faster access times and better reliability.

• Data Archiving: Data archiving involves storing infrequently accessed data in a cost-effective manner. This process is similar to how the brain prunes unnecessary synaptic connections and retains only relevant information.

• Backup and Recovery: Backup systems ensure data integrity and availability by creating copies of data that can be restored in case of data loss. This mirrors the brain's ability to consolidate and reconsolidate memories, ensuring that important information is retained and accessible.

Analogies and Insights:

The parallels between biological memory systems and engineering memory mechanisms offer valuable insights for both fields. Understanding how the brain efficiently stores, retrieves, and processes information can inspire new approaches in computer architecture and database design. Conversely, advancements in engineering memory systems can provide models for understanding and simulating cognitive processes.

For instance, the brain's ability to prioritize and filter relevant information through attention mechanisms can inform the design of more efficient caching algorithms. Similarly, the concept of memory consolidation and reconsolidation can inspire new methods for data backup, recovery, and optimization in engineering systems.

Furthermore, the dynamic nature of memory in the brain, where synaptic connections are continuously modified and refined, can inspire adaptive memory systems in engineering. These systems could dynamically adjust their caching strategies and storage hierarchies based on changing workloads and access patterns, improving overall efficiency and performance.

4.4 Transfer Learning:

Considered as one of the powerful methodologies in machine learning, transfer learning practices the knowledge gained in one task to perform well in a relative but different task. This is of greater advantage in cases where data scarcity exists and even in adapting models to new environments. Furthermore, fine-tuning and reusing of the pre-trained models under transfer learning remarkably reduce the necessities of resourceful training data and computational cost; therefore, this is time-effective and an efficient approach for numerous engineering applications. The section that follows will detail the transfer learning techniques that apply to engineering tasks because, more often than not, they require new environmental settings; very limited or no data compatible with the task under consideration are available.

- **Transfer Learning Approaches in Engineering**

The main idea of transfer learning is that knowledge learned for solving one problem can be transferred to another problem also, more so if they share some common features and structures. Basically, there are two steps involved in this process:

Pre-training: The initial training of the model on a large representative corpus of the target task. By going through this process, the model learns representations engaging small and importable meaning, which it will be able to perform on future related tasks.

Fine-tuning: Pre-trained network adapted to a new task by training it using a smaller task-specific dataset. This process is guided on how an original pre-trained model parameter can be fine-tuned to optimize the general performance for the new task and not lose previous knowledge built during pre-training.

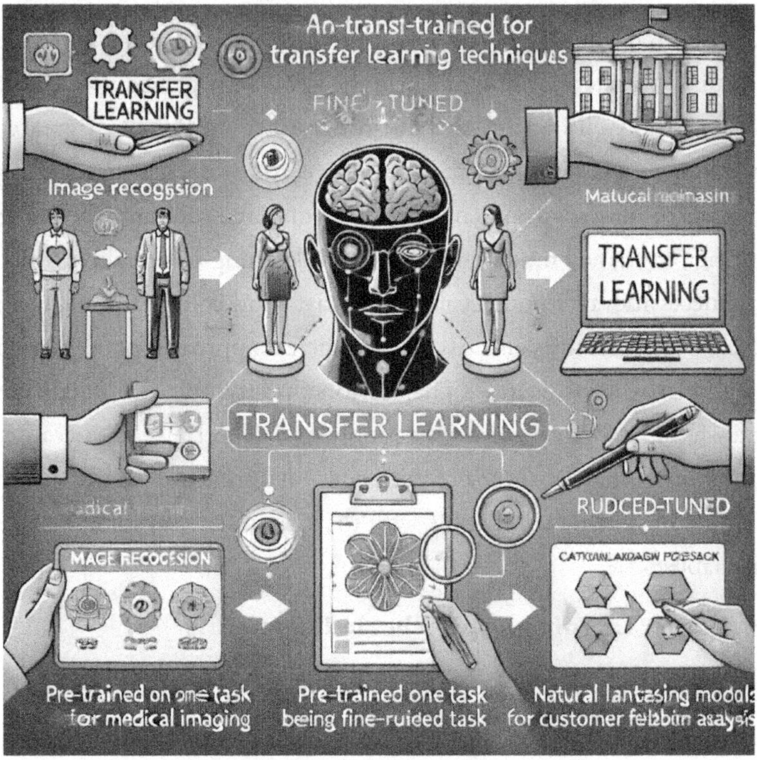

Figure 4.4: Transfer Learning Techniques

This illustration depicts transfer learning techniques, showing a model pre-trained on one task being fine-tuned for another related task. Examples include image recognition being adapted to medical imaging and natural language processing models being adapted for customer feedback analysis. The diagram highlights the efficiency and reduced training data required.

- **Transfer Learning Techniques**

The process of transfer learning applies several techniques while adapting a pre-trained model towards learning new tasks.

Feature Extraction: This process uses the feature extraction layers of the pre-trained model to process a new dataset. The final classification layer is altered and retrained on this new data. The model learns the overall features, which are usually fast in pre-training, thereby helping the model adapt to the new job very quickly.

Fine-tuning: This is achieved by retraining some or all of the layers in a pre-trained model with a new dataset. In general, it is expected that the first few layers will become non-trainable or frozen, i.e., its parameters will no longer be updated, whereas the later layers that extract higher-level features will be simply fine-tuned. This fine-tuning approach balances retention of general knowledge with adaptation to the specifics of the new task.

Domain Adaptation: This is the study of techniques that adapt a pre-trained model from one domain with a particular distribution to a new domain with a different data distribution. The approaches fundamentally reduce a mismatched representation by adapting a model to minimize the difference between the source domain, where the model has had its pre-training, and a target domain where the model would be applied. They come in different shades where one trains the model to know how best to differentiate source from target domain data and adjusts its parameters with this knowledge.

Multi-Task Learning: Multi-task learning refers to the training of a model on more than one task simultaneously. In that sense, by learning from commonalities shared between tasks, all the tasks can be improved together. Consequently, the transfer learning derived from the model will be stronger and better in driving better performance.

Transfer learning is a useful technique and applicable to several engineering tasks that require high utility values, especially in cases where adaptability to new environments or tasks, along with learning on limited data, is a requirement. A few concrete examples are as follows:

Transfer learning significantly transformed image recognition tasks within various fields, particularly autonomous vehicles, medical imaging, and industrial inspection. For example, a model pre-trained on a large dataset in a certain domain can be fine-tuned for defect detection in manufacturing or for medical condition diagnosis utilizing radiographic imaging. The pre-trained models can thus achieve relatively high accuracies because of the use of high-level feature representations.

Natural Language Processing: Transfer learning is an interesting aspect as it applies to natural language processing when applied to task variations, such as sentiment analysis, machine translation, and text summarization. Pre-trained models like BERT and GPT-3 are fine-tuned across large text corpora within different domain classes for further fine-tuning towards applications that include, for example, the analysis of customer feedback or automated report generation. This significantly reduces the data and training time needed to achieve high performance for such applications.

Robotics and Autonomous Systems: Transfer learning can be used for enabling the robots and autonomous systems to automatically come up with new situations and functions. For example, a robot, trained with a specific surrounding setup for navigation, will apply its learned navigation capability to some new environment that looks the same, with possibly little training sometimes. This has direct application in rescue missions in which the robot has to adapt to a changing environment or topography.

Predictive Maintenance: Transfer learning can be used to carry out predictive maintenance of machinery and equipment. However, it is possible to fine-tune models pre-trained with data from similar machineries to predict failures and maintenance needs for a machine or equipment that shall have meager historical data about it. This will increase the reliability and operation efficiency of the maintenance, and reduce downtime and costs.

One main area where transfer learning has been applied is in the processing of speech and audio, such as speech recognition, identification of speakers, and acoustic event detection. In speech, it can even extend to fine-tuning pretrained models over large-scale speech datasets, to recognize, for example, accents or certain dialects, or even audio events toward better robustness and accuracy of speech-based systems across a wide variety of environments.

Environmental Monitoring: Transfer learning can be used to develop models, component monitoring, and prediction of environmental changes. Therefore, a satellite pre-trained model can be fine-tuned in detecting environmental phenomena of interest, such as deforestation, urban expansion, and pollution levels.

Healthcare and Biomedical Engineering: Transfer learning plays a great role in healthcare and biomedical engineering. Pre-trained models, using large medical datasets, can be fine-tuned specifically for a diagnostic task—for example, the detection of a rare disease or extraction of features from medical images. This helps in solving the poor availability of data for rare cases problem and, therefore, in turn, brings about improvements in diagnosis, eventually helping in improving patient care.

Transfer learning has many pluses, but at the same time it poses several challenges and considerations:

Domain Differences: Transfer learning works fine only when the source and target domains are reasonably similar. Drastic differences in both the distributions of data and the feature representations between the two domains are some of the potential limiting factors of the power of boosting one model's performance with the aid of transfer learning. The existing differences with the target domain have to be catered to through domain adaptation techniques.

Overfitting: Since a pre-trained model is fine-tuned with the data, there is the risk of overfitting, where the model characterizes new data from its specificity, losing the capability of generalization. This will be the major effect of regularization techniques, like dropout and weight decay, which the model does not depend much on data for fine-tuning.

Computational Resources: Computation resources required for transfer learning to relax on vast training data at times should be quite a handsome lot for fine-tuning pre-trained models. For this reason, it requires access to powerful hardware like GPUs or TPUs in order to be done efficiently.

Interpretability: In transfer learning, more so with deep neural networks, it is not quite an easy task to interpret the working phases of knowledge transfer and the reused or fine-tuned features used in transparency and trust for AI systems. This is something where the techniques of model interpretability and explain ability come to play.

Ethical and Fairness Considerations: The use of pre-trained models automatically propagates the bias of the source data. Transferring fairness and ethical considerations into the model would, therefore, require careful evaluation of the pre-trained model itself and the fine-tuning process. The inclusion of bias detection and mitigation techniques within the transfer learning workflow is needed.

4.5 Forgetting and Remembering:

Just like in biological and artificial systems, forgetting and remembering occur naturally. They play a key role in the management and use of information. In biological and human systems, these processes facilitate adaptive behavior, efficiency in learning, and cognitive flexibility. In artificial systems, it may be imposed to provide adaptability, robustness, and efficiency. In this chapter, such mechanisms are deeply explored and provided on engineering systems.

This diagram illustrates mechanisms of forgetting and remembering in both biological and artificial systems. It highlights processes like synaptic pruning and long-term depression (LTD) in the brain, and regularization and dropout in artificial systems. The diagram also shows the implications for robustness and adaptability in engineering systems.

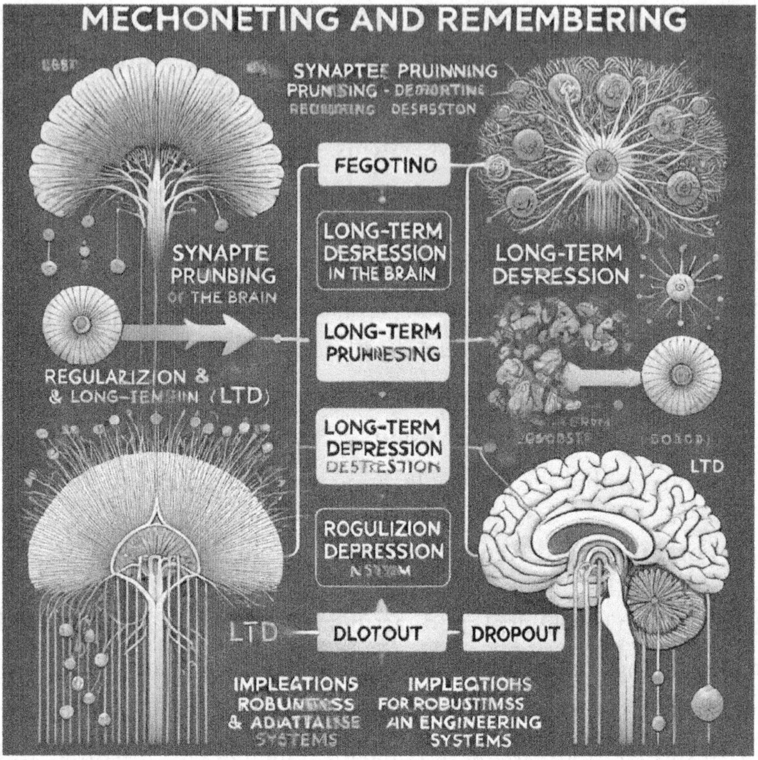

Figure 4.5: Mechanisms of Forgetting and Remembering

Biological Mechanisms of Forgetting and Remembering

Dynamic processes of forgetting and remembering in the human brain involve multiple neural and biochemical mechanisms. The very same processes ensure vast efficiency and adaptability on the brain's part to focus only on what is relevant from the information, shunning the irrelevant.

Forgetting is thus not mere inability but an active tool that could serve most important functions one would imagine. A major mechanism through which brain may forget is by a process referred to as synaptic pruning. This elimination allows for more efficient neural circuits to form, which in turn allows for a more efficient functioning of the brain by allowing it to focus on the most relevant connections. Other mechanisms of weakening involve long-term synaptic depression, short for LTD. LTD balances LTP so the synapses do not grow too strong and saturated with all kind of irrelevant stuff. Such a balance is important to cognitive flexibility, as it avoids overload.

Reminding recalls string information stored. Recall can also be classified into types of memory systems such as short-term and long-term memory. STM is one that only allows the holding and manipulation of information for a short moment; for instance, the number somebody remembers just enough time when it is dialed. The duration meant to be assigned to the stored information runs from hours through a lifetime in the LTM. However, a key process to remember is memory consolidation, where the content in STM is transferred to LTM. The process of making new memories fit into the old neural network structure is called memory consolidation. Most of this process occurs when we are sleeping. The role of the hippocampus in memory consolidation is to transfer the information into the neocortex for eventual storage. The information storage can be retrieved, and the information accessed can then be reconsolidated, possibly modified, and strengthened thereafter. This dynamically copes with memories being relevant and moldable toward new information, hence allows learning and adaptation.

Artificial Mechanisms of Forgetting and Remembering

Artificial systems have mechanisms of forgetting and remembering incorporated within them to ensure data management, which through that implements efficient models eliciting high performance and remains adaptive toward novel tasks and environment changes.

The process of forgetting in artificial systems may either be intentional or an aftereffect of some form of random processes. The idea of intentional forgetting can be realized through regularization, dropout, and weight decay. These methods avoid overfitting with the approach of simplifying the model and not allowing much dependence on small training data details. In an effective sense, regularization techniques allow the model to generalize reasonably over new data; therefore, the model would gain robustness and adaptability. Cache eviction policies and such can also be applied in managing memory so that less relevant data declines in order to dispose of it for more room with more relevant data. This is very similar to the concept in the brain where underused connections get eliminated in a process called synaptic pruning to enhance efficiency.

Memory in artificial systems derives itself based on what it means to store and retrieve information. This is effected using a combination of concepts that are inclusive of caching, database management, and model storage. Basically, the architecture of a computer with regard to memory includes mechanisms that cache commonly used data in order to be retrieved fast. For example, it caches data in L1, L2, and L3, following the scheme for organizing data by relevance, just like the short-term memory of the human brain. Just like the human brain can remember, database systems are optimized regarding their indexing and query. Artificial neural networks will store the knowledge provided as modeled parameters. Transfer learning and fine-tuning methods let these models remember and adapt past knowledge applied to a new task, which then enhances performance with rather little extra training.

Implications for Engineering Systems

The mechanisms of forgetting and remembering have great implications for the robustness and adaptability of engineering systems. Knowledge for designing systems that can operate with high efficiency, be adaptable, and perform complex tasks can be engineered based on understanding the mechanisms and principles. Intentional forgetting mechanisms, such as regularization and cache eviction policies, increase the robustness of systems engineering. It does not lead to overfitting; the straight consequence of it is the guarantee of good generalization of the model to new data and new environments. Industrial applications benefit from such a robust system by enabling performance and maintaining reliability under changing working conditions that often result in the main reason for system breakdown and nonproducing times.

Mechanisms of remembrance, such as transfer learning and fine-tuning, allow systems in engineering to adapt quickly and efficiently to new tasks and environments. For instance, in the domain of autonomous driving, one can pre-train a model on the available driving data and then fine-tune in other geographic regions; that would imply little additional training is needed for the vehicle to be ready for new conditions. Effective memory management inspired by biological processes such as synaptic pruning will ensure that realized engineering systems allocate resources efficiently. Therefore, with such efficient caching and memory management, computer architecture is able to reduce latencies and improve performances such that a system will be able to manage data and quickly respond to it.

Memory is dynamical in nature; that is, it must be able to change constantly at the biological and the artificial levels. Online learning or reinforcement learning in these artificial systems is accomplished with the help of paradigms that help models re-update knowledge based on the data and feedback provided to it. Such balance for the learning paradigm is important for the effective application of real-time monitoring, predictive maintenance, and adaptive control systems. Striking a balance like this would mean the design of an effective data management strategy. Efficient indexing and query optimization in database systems help achieve on-time access to information, whereas the strategies of archiving and backup ensure the integrity of data. These would be very important in applications like financial analysis, management of healthcare, and scientific research.

The principles of forgetting and remembering can further be a trigger to improvement in the engineering system, based on the scaling of that system. Current systems achieve their scalability from effective management of memory and learning mechanisms. Like in scalable cloud computing, caching and load balancing dynamically manage resources for both performance and high availability. The systems that associate a science of forgetting and remembering are best fit to face the various changes and distractions. This capacity to self-modify and further tune cognitive Knowledge makes them effective in adapting to new challenges and recovering from failures. In applications such as critical disaster response and cybersecurity, the degree of resilience is important to ensure reliability and effectiveness.

In consumer applications, effective memory management benefits the user experience through quick accesses to relevant information, having also the ability to adapt to user preferences. For example, e-commerce and streaming recommendation systems make use of memory mechanisms in providing personalized content recommendation to enhance user satisfaction and engagement. In other words, the mechanism of forgetting and remembering in biosystems provides valuable inspiration for designing solid, adaptive, and efficient engineering systems. Applying those understandings will enable engineers to grow AI technologies and data management strategies that will boost performance, scalability, and resilience for applications. The ongoing refinement of such mechanisms in artificial systems holds even greater potential and an unlimited impact on driving innovation and enhancing outcomes in diverse areas.

5

Consciousness and Artificial General Intelligence (AGI)

Consciousness and Artificial General Intelligence are arguably the deepest and most challenging frontiers facing neuroscience and artificial intelligence, respectively, today. Consciousness, meaning the state or quality of being aware of one's condition and surroundings, delineates the most central of human life experiences. It forms the basis for thoughts, feelings, and perceptions and, as such, propels our acting and interaction within the world. The quest to understand consciousness has been intriguing to philosophers, scholars, and scientist for ages by questioning the nature of self-awareness and the very essence of being human.

Whereas Artificial General Intelligence is defined as developing machines able to understand, learn, and use knowledge in a wide spectrum of tasks at a level matching human intelligence. Unlike narrow AI, which is good at language or image recognition, AGI aims to devise systems that generalize learning across many disciplines. Instead, AGI is the aspiration to develop machines able to do anything a human can do—potentially revolutionizing every area of life: health, education, production, and entertainment.

The present chapter deals with the complicated relationship between consciousness and AGI, whereby the theories of consciousness and their pertinence are probed with respect to artificial systems. In particular, the ethical and philosophical repercussions of creating a machine that eventually turns conscious or forms some of it are looked upon. We will give an overview of the difficulties and milestones in the quest for AGI, showing both the potential benefits and risks that come with such powerful technology. The purpose of the work is to provide the audience with a clear introduction as to where exactly the current research lies, and which future trends are going to take us closer to the aim of developing truly intelligent machines.

5.1 What is Consciousness?

This diagram illustrates the understanding of consciousness, showing the brain regions involved (such as the thalamus, cortex, and hippocampus) and their functions. It includes aspects of the global workspace theory and integrated information theory.

Consciousness is a very interesting and most difficult phenomenon to understand in neuroscience, psychology, philosophy, and artificial intelligence. In essence, consciousness is the state of being aware of and being able to think of oneself and environment. It ranges along experiences; it may be in form of sensory perception and emotion to self-awareness and reflective thought. Research in consciousness focuses on the nature, origin, mechanism, and how it all relates to Artificial Intelligence (AI) and the problems of creating Artificial General Intelligence(AGI).

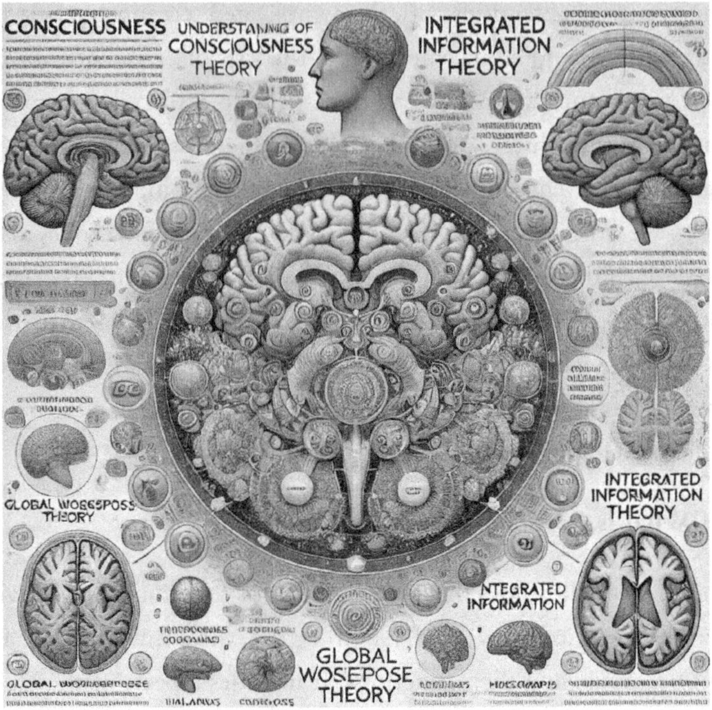

Figure 5.1: Understanding Consciousness

The Nature of Consciousness

Consciousness is usually divided into two broad components: phenomenal consciousness and access consciousness. Phenomenal consciousness refers to the subjective experience of being aware, often described as "what it feels like" to have certain experiences. This comprises sensory experiences and qualities of emotional states and thoughts. Cognitive access consciousness, however, involves the access to information and the means to act on it, both with respect to reasoning and making decisions, and reporting, through that aspect of consciousness that makes possible the guided and intended operation of mental states.

Another key distinction is that between the state and the process of consciousness. The former can be combined with degrees, ranging from fully awake to several stages of sleep, coma, or anesthesia. As a process, consciousness refers to the dynamic activity of interplay between distinct neural systems necessary for the integration of sensory information, maintenance Attention, and generation of self-awareness.

Theories of Consciousness

A number of theories have been forwarded in describing the mechanisms behind consciousness. These theories intend to look for the neuro correlates of the experience of consciousness, which are the neural aspects that exclusively correlate in one way or another with the state of consciousness in the brain.

Global Workspace Theory: Bernard Baars is the proponent of this theory, founded on the premise that consciousness is conceived by the very integration of information within a 'global workspace' somewhere inside the brain. The 'global workspace' is considered a network of neurons broadcasting information to different regions of the brain, which distribute and further process the content. According to GWT, information becomes a conscious state when it is transmitted to this global workspace in the brain and quickly becomes available for higher-order cognitive functions such as reasoning, decision-making, and verbal reporting.

Integrated Information Theory: Proposed by Giulio Tononi, IIT states that the [.] level of consciousness represents a measure of how much integrated information is available in the brain at any given time. Indeed, the information level is determined by an integrated level of the information that has to be quantified in the system and can be measured via "phi" (Φ). Higher values of Φ pertain to states of greater consciousness. The IIT proposes that this is because complex interactions between neural networks allow very diverse information to be integrated into one unique experience.

It is the recurrent processing theory—RPT—which Victor Lamme proposed. RPT emphasizes that recurrent or feedback connections in the brain are most relevant to the experience of consciousness. RPT says that consciousness is involved when, instead of just fed-forward information from the senses, what is fed forward is reworked in recurrent loops through areas higher in the hierarchy. By this action, information from the senses may be held on to and analyzed in fine detail, leading to conscious perception.

Higher-Order Theories: According to HOT, consciousness emerges from higher-order representations of mental states. In other words, these theories hypothesize that the mental state becomes conscious if it is represented by another mental state, but one of a higher order. Such a kind of process of self-reference allows an individual to be aware of what is going on in his mind and experiences. HOTs stress the contribution of metacognition, simply 'thinking about thinking,' to the generation of conscious awareness.

Attention Schema Theory: Provided in part by Michael Graziano, AST puts forth that there is consciousness arising from this internal schema of attention maintained in the brain. That is, AST maintains the notion that the brain creates a model of its processes of attention. That is what can control and guide surveillance hence the subjective experience of being aware of something. AST postulates that consciousness is an adaptive mechanism, aimed to improve brain concentration on informational developments and decision-making.

The Neural Basis of Consciousness:

More specifically, an understanding of the neural basis of consciousness should go hand in hand with the identification of brain regions or networks for which activity generates conscious experience. It appears that research has never succeeded in finding a single point of the brain that could be associated with conscious experience; it looks more like coordinated activity across a wide variety of locations in the brain.

The Thalamocortical System: The thalamus and the cerebral cortex form the central elements of most theories of consciousness. The thalamus acts as a relay center, forwarding all incoming sensory information to the cortex for higher processing. The thalamocortical system, composed of reciprocal projections between the thalamus and the various cortical areas, is responsible for gaining the sensory signals and the performance of acts of consciousness.

Default mode network is a put-together of brain regions, medial prefrontal cortex, posterior cingulate cortex, and angular gyrus, involved in rest and self-referential thought. The DMN seems to have a role in processes connected with the introspective states of one's functioning, autobiographical memory, and mind-wandering. Disruptions in the activity of the DMN have been related to dissimilar states of consciousness, including sleep, anesthesia, and psychiatric disorders.

Anatomically, the most eminent roles of these regions are in the regulation of attention, emotional awareness, and interoceptive awareness. The ACC and insula are part of the salience network, which helps to order preference for attention and distribute it accordingly. Activity in these areas is related to the subjective experience of emotions and bodily sensations, thus adding to the richness of conscious experience.

The Prefrontal Cortex: The prefrontal cortex is engaged in high-order cognitive functions such as decision-making, planning, and executive control. It has also been used for metacognitive processes and the formation of high-order representations of mental states. Lesions in the prefrontal cortex manifest associated with disturbances of self-awareness and conscious control of behavior.

Consciousness and Artificial Intelligence

The quest for an understanding of consciousness has important implications for the development of artificial intelligence and the quest for AGI. Even today, the capabilities of today's artificial intelligence systems are tremendous in narrow areas, while they surprise with their generality and flexibility. Truly attaining AGI would require the creation of systems that learn and adapt as easily across a very broad spectrum of tasks as humans do. Therefore, an understanding toward the facts of consciousness may give insights into how to develop machines having the same abilities.

Machine Consciousness: It has also been argued that as we understand and replicate the machinery of consciousness in machines, we will achieve machine consciousness. This entails engineering AI systems, not just for the purpose of doing work, but also for performing meaningful self-reflections on themselves. The entire concept of machine consciousness raises several dilemmas both in cognitive and philosophical speeches about selfhood, agency, and moral responsibility.

Ethical Concerns: Consciousness or consciousness-like features of artificial intelligence systems suggest immense ethical concerns. In the potential case that machines probably evolve to a definite state of consciousness, it should be thought about their rights and their treatment. In addition, they are predicted to eventually do business more effectively than humans, thus requiring discussions on employment, privacy, and social structure changes.

Empowering AI with Consciousness-like Capabilities: Even though full machine consciousness lies beyond our reach today, features inspired by consciousness inserted into AI systems can augment their efficiency and adaptability. For example, AI systems designed with better mechanisms of attention and metacognitive and self-monitoring skills can enhance their efficiency at work and flexibility in complex environments.

5.2 Artificial Consciousness

Artificial consciousness, more commonly known as machine or synthetic consciousness, discusses the possibility of machines having forms of awareness or subjective experience. While existing artificial intelligence systems have managed to realize intricate operations and highly advanced problem-solving, they are still devoid of self-awareness and subjective experiences propounded by human consciousness. In this section, the theoretical underpinning, possible mechanisms, and value issues are probed in artificial consciousness.

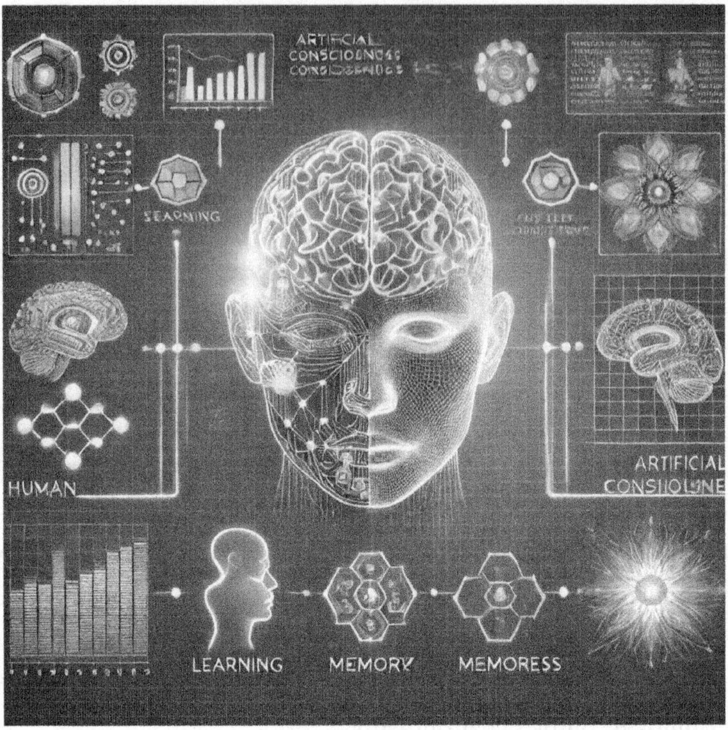

Figure 5.2: Artificial Consciousness

This conceptual illustration of artificial consciousness depicts a comparison between a human brain and an artificial neural network. It highlights the parallels in structure and function, including aspects like learning, memory, and self-awareness.

Artificial consciousness lies at the intersection of cognitive science, neuroscience, philosophy of mind, and artificial intelligence. Much of the theoretical debate is driven by the core set of questions: what is the nature of consciousness, and can processes associated with it be mechanized? Philosophers and scientists offer a number of definitions, ranging from simple awareness to complexly self-reflective thought. A closely related question is whether mechanization of the processes producing human consciousness is feasible, i.e., whether emulation of biological neural processes is possible using silicon-based systems. If consciousness is the product of particular patterns of information processing, then it would seem possible for machines to implement these patterns. Functionalism, a theory in the philosophy of mind, considers mental states to be defined by their functional roles, and not by physical substrates. This view posits that if a machine could do what a conscious being does, then it would be conscious, as functionality is prioritized over material makeup.

Several models for artificial consciousness have been put forward, taking inspiration from biological systems and progress in artificial intelligence and computational neuroscience. The performance of artificial neural networks—especially deep learning models—has been exemplary in tasks such as image recognition, natural language processing, and playing games. Some researchers believe that the increasing complexity and depth of these networks holds out hope for systems that depict conscious behaviors. Bernard Baars' Global Workspace Theory (GWT) claims that consciousness arises from integrating information in a global workspace within the brain, and this theory can apply to artificial consciousness through the implementation of global workspace architecture in machines. Integrated Information Theory (IIT) by Giulio Tononi postulates that the degree of information integration within a system corresponds to its level of consciousness. Architectures that maximize information integration could potentially produce conscious-like states. Recurrent neural networks (RNNs) and other architectures with feedback loops, which process sequences and retain information over time, might be important in building machines that analyze sensory input similarly to the brain. Attention mechanisms in systems like Transformers enable them to focus on relevant parts of the input data, improving their selective processing ability, which is important in conscious experience.

Developing artificial consciousness gives rise to important ethical and philosophical questions. If machines were to become conscious, their moral status and rights would have to be taken into account. Conscious machines might suffer or enjoy well-being, prompting debate on their treatment and ethical use. Issues of responsibility and accountability will also arise concerning the actions of conscious machines. The societal impact of conscious machines could be significant, affecting industry, employment, privacy, and social structures. Ensuring the benefits of artificial consciousness are equitably distributed and addressing existential risks, such as super-intelligent machines potentially threatening humankind, are critical considerations. Ensuring that the development of artificial consciousness is safe and beneficial remains a major challenge.

Research on artificial consciousness is in its infancy, with many questions still open. Several promising avenues of investigation are being pursued by scientists and engineers. Computational models simulating neural processes can provide insights into the emergence of consciousness in artificial systems. Brain-machine interface systems, linking human brains with artificial systems, may inform the nature of consciousness and eventually lead to the development of machines displaying conscious-like behavior. Interdisciplinary integration, involving neuroscientists, computer scientists, philosophers, and ethicists, is crucial for advancing this field. Ethical frameworks must be developed to regulate and guide the responsible development and use of artificial consciousness, ensuring ethical issues are addressed in its design and deployment.

Artificial consciousness holds a fascinating and challenging frontier status in Artificial Intelligence and Cognitive Science. Understanding the nature of consciousness and the mechanisms that might replicate it in machines requires cross-fertilization of ideas and a deep appreciation of the associated ethical and philosophical implications. While the actualization of true artificial consciousness may still be a distant prospect, pursuing this objective will significantly alter our understanding of intelligence and self-awareness, blurring the lines between humans and machines. As research progresses, it is crucial to navigate the ethical terrain thoughtfully, ensuring that the development of artificial consciousness aligns with human values and supports societal well-being.

5.3 The Quest for AGI

Artificial General Intelligence is the new frontier in artificial intelligence research, geared toward the creation of machines that understand, learn, and apply knowledge like human beings across a wide spectrum of tasks. Whereas narrow AI excels in the different specific domains—from languages to image recognition—AGI seeks a degree of intelligence based on the generalization of learning, so that it can perform any intellectual task which a human is capable of performing. The quest toward AGI is in no way linked to a purely technological problem but envelopes a strictly scientific and deeply philosophical approach, one raising basic questions about the nature of intelligence, consciousness, and the resulting future for human-machine interactions.

Development of AGI will involve a few key aspects: developing algorithms that learn with limited data, design of systems that allow transfer learning across different domains, and mechanisms to be applied so that machines adapt to newer and totally unforeseen challenges. Said another way, achieving AGI will require probably breakthroughs in a rather broad range of topics related to machine learning, neurosciences, cognitive science, and robotics.

Figure 5.3: The Quest for AGI

This illustration shows the quest for Artificial General Intelligence (AGI). It includes elements like advanced neural networks, learning algorithms, and cognitive architectures. It highlights applications such as robotics, natural language processing, and autonomous systems.

Learning and Adaptation in AGI

Among the most significant challenges in the development of AGI is designing learning algorithms that will generalize well across many tasks and environments. The AI systems of today need vast amounts of data and extensive training to give excellent performance on specialized tasks. Human intelligence, on the other hand, is spectacularly flexible and efficient about learning from limited data and transferring knowledge across a wide range of domains. AGI research has focused its efforts on the development of more formidable and powerful learning algorithms and architectures.

Meta-Learning: The meta-learning approach seeks to develop models that are able to adapt to new tasks quickly from limited data. The learning algorithms of meta-learning get trained on a distribution of tasks rather than on a single task to enable the extraction of common patterns and principles related to all tasks and hence apply on new tasks. Model-agnostic meta-learning and RNNs applied for meta-learning have been able to demonstrate fast adaptation and generalization.

Few-Shot and Zero-Shot Learning: Few-shot learning is when a model learns to transfer to new tasks with very few examples, while a scenario in which the model is expected to generalize to tasks that it has never seen before is zero-shot learning. Basically, both the approaches are a takeoff to the remarkable human ability to learn new concepts and skills upon exposure, which could be very limited. shemale Thus, techniques designed to boost few-shot and zero-shot learning include Siamese networks, memory-augmented neural networks, and semantic embeddings.

Transfer Learning: Transfer learning refers to using models trained on one task and then tuning them further for another related task. This has much more manageable requirements in terms of training data and computational resources, hence a practical technique to achieve AGI. This is applied in applications like image recognition, natural language processing, and medical diagnosis.

Cognitive Architectures and AGI

AGI requires cognitive architectures designed to be flexible and adaptive, emulating man's cognition. Cognitive architectures could be computational frameworks that attempt to model the underlying human thought processes and behavior. In a manner, such architectures are capable of bringing a number of cognitive functions together, including perception, memory, learning, reasoning, and decision-making to come up with systems capable of intelligent behavior.

Soar: Soar is a cognitive architecture that models human cognition with the aid of a production rule system. It integrates various cognitive functions along with learning mechanisms to imitate human problem-solving and decision-making processes. Soar has been applied to a number of different applications, including robotics, natural language processing, and intelligent tutoring systems.

ACT-R: Adaptive Control of Thought-Rational is a cognitive architecture centered on the theory of rational behavior in modeling human cognition. It merges declarative memory, which is concerned with facts and knowledge, and procedural memory, which concerns skills and actions, in an effort to closely simulate human cognitive processes. It has been applied in human-computer interaction, cognitive psychology, and educational technology, among other areas.

NARS: Non-Axiomatic Reasoning System is a cognitive architecture concentrated on adaptive reasoning and learning. Because it is able to deal with uncertainty, incomplete knowledge, and changing environments, it is suitable for AGI. It uses a unified framework to integrate a wide array of different higher-level cognitive functions, such as perception, memory, learning, and decision-making.

Embodiment and AGI

Another important component of AGI is embodiment, which means it would have a physical presence and interaction with one's environment. Human intelligence is deeply rooted in our physical interactions with the world, where essential sensory and motor experiences are derived. Artificial intelligence in the form of an embodied agent aims to replicate these features by incorporating physical bodies with sensory inputs in the learning and decision-making process.

Robotics provides AI systems with a platform of embodiment, hence offering the most essential part in the quest for AGI. Equipped with sensors, actuators, and sophisticated control systems, robots are able to interact with the physical world, learn from experiences, and adapt to new challenges. In this vein, advances in robotics, especially soft robotics, bio-inspired designs, and multimodal sensors, offer opportunities for developing more complexly embodied AGI systems.

Virtual Environments: Another approach to embodiment is virtual environments. In these virtual environments, rich and very interactive simulations are provided to the AI systems. Such systems enable AI to experience a very wide range of situations without being confined by constrained physical hardware. Virtual reality and augmented reality further increase the realism and sophistication of such an environment, providing ease in developing AGI.

Human-robot interaction: HRI revolves around the interaction with the robot; the major emphases of this research area are on collaboration, communication, and social understanding. Relevant progress in natural language processing, emotion recognition, and social cognition has to be made for the development of meaningful HRI-capable AGI.

The quest to achieve Artificial General Intelligence is multidisciplinary, multifaceted, and very ambitious. Constructing machines possessing general intelligence comparable to human beings builds on advances to learning algorithms, cognitive architectures, embodiment, and ethical considerations. Though so much ground was covered on this journey towards AGI, the struggle continues, driven by the vision of creating intelligent systems that will transform society, enhancing the capability of Man.

5.4 Ethical and Social Implications

Such development in Artificial General Intelligence thus goes with deep ethical and social implications that transcend technological growth. The closer we get to developing machines possessing the capabilities of general intelligence, the more important it will be to consider possible impacts on society, individual rights, and ethical standards. To this effect, this chapter reviews the ethical and social dimensions associated with AGI: bias, fairness, accountability, job displacement, and other broader implications for society in general.

Figure 5.4: Ethical and Social Implications of AGI

This diagram illustrates the ethical and social implications of AGI. It shows aspects such as bias and fairness, accountability, job displacement, privacy, and societal impact. Symbols or icons represent each of these issues.

Bias and Fairness

Bias and injustices in the decision-making process top the list of ethical issues with AGI. AI, including AGI, is usually trained on really large datasets that often bear the impress of historical biases and sins of society. If these are not dealt with, AGI will strengthen these discriminatory practices in areas like hiring, lending, law enforcement, and healthcare.

Fairness in AGI requires developing algorithms and training practices that not only avoid bias but make efforts to mitigate it. This shall include techniques that will be in a position to detect and correct biases in training data and models. This would, therefore, involve the usage of fairness-aware algorithms, regular audits, and correction against bias so that AI guarantees equality in decisions.

- **Diverse and Representative Data**: Ensuring that the datasets used for training are both diverse and representative of the populations and contexts in which the deployment of AGI systems is intended has the effect of reducing the probability of AI systems treating underrepresented groups unfairly.

- **Transparency and Explainability**: Development of transparent and explainable AGI systems about their decision-making processes. On the other hand, transparency allows the user to understand how decisions are made, while explainability enables stakeholders to identify and therefore try to avoid possible biases.

Accountability and Responsibility

As the level of system autonomy and capabilities increases, so do questions about accountability and responsibility. Who is culpable for AGI acts and decisions? gets more and more pressing, thus underlining the issues related to legal responsibility, moral accountability, and liability in case of harm or other significant decisions made by AGI systems.

Accountability Frameworks are finally clear:

- **Legal and Regulatory Frameworks**: The need is pressing for laws and regulations that inform roles, responsibilities, and liabilities for developers, users, and proprietors of AGI systems; they should clearly state the negligent behavior, malfunction, and misuse of AGI technology.

- **Ethical Guidelines and Codes of Conduct**: The development of ethical guidelines and codes of conduct for the development of AGI requires setting out the ethical principles that should guide research in and use of AGI, taking into account that ethical considerations should be fused into the development processes.

- **Oversight and Governance**: Developing oversight mechanisms and governance structures that track the development and fielding of AGI systems in terms of their initiation, execution, and completion. This includes the establishment of independent review boards, ethical committees, and regulatory agencies that shall preside over the ethical implications of AGI.

Job Displacement and Economic Impact

Its full-scale diffusion may have significant effects on the job market and, more generally, on the economy. AGI systems will then be able to automate very large ranges of tasks, entailing loss of jobs and changes in the nature of work. While mechanization has increased productivity and hence economic growth throughout history, it also gives way to concerns about unemployment, income inequality, and social disruption.

Addressing the economic impact of AGI requires:

- **Workforce Transition and Retraining**: Putting in place policies and programs for the transferring workforce into new jobs and industries by means of retraining and upskilling, with a view to adjusting to the changing job market.

- **Universal Basic Income (UBI)**: A way to be ensured of at least some degree of financial security in a future with higher automation, UBI could help alleviate the economic blow of job loss by ensuring individuals have a basic level of income irrespective of employment status.

- **Inclusive Growth and Innovation**: Promote inclusive growth and innovation by encouraging new industries and jobs that are going to have a use for the AGI technology. This includes nurturing entrepreneurship and links to small businesses in the market while investing in sectors likely to garner new employment opportunities.

Privacy and Surveillance

Development and deployment of AGI systems raise large concerns about privacy and surveillance. For example, AGI systems processing very vast amounts of data can be used in person-to-person and group activity monitoring, creating the likelihood for infringement on privacy rights and civil liberties. Ensuring that AGI technology is respectful to privacy and used responsibly is one of the important ethical questions.

Privacy Protection and Misuse Prevention:

- **Data Protection and Privacy Laws**: These are rigid laws, to be enacted on data protection and privacy in regard to the collection, storage, and utilization of personal data by the AGI system. Such laws must ensure that the person retains control over the data and is protected from intrusion into his or her private life.

• **Ethical Use of Data**: Advocating for good practices of ethical data use in consent, transparency, and reduction of data collection; AGI systems must be designed for privacy by default and should incorporate privacy-enhancing technologies.

• **Surveillance Oversight**: To have in place better oversight mechanisms that provide monitoring and regulation for AGI systems used for conducting surveillance, including the setting up of independent oversight entities that keep track of governmental and corporate surveillance activities to ensure that practices are ethical and legally compliant.

Societal Impact and Ethical Considerations

The societal impact of AGI surpasses individual ethical issues and moves to broader ones involving the potential for AGI to transform social structures, influence human behavior, and shape cultural norms. With the realization and incorporation of AGI systems into society, long-term impacts on human relationships, social cohesion, and cultural values all become challenging to consider.

Societal Impacts:

• **Public Engagement and Dialogue**: Engaging society with issues of an ethical and social nature that surround the emergence of AGI through free, informed, and open dialogue and raising awareness, aiming at engaging diverse stakeholders in decision-making processes.

• **Ethical Education and Literacy**: Encourages ethical education and literacy to let people understand the probable consequences of AGI and help them choose ethically in terms of using the system. This also includes that the education which would be based on STEM would be made ethical, and resources would be provided for reflection upon ethics and debate.

- **Cultural Sensitivity and Inclusivity**: Make sure that the development and deployment of AGI are culturally sensitive and inclusive, recognizing and valuing a variety of cultural perspectives and values, so that AGI systems are inclusive and accessible to all members of society.

The development of AGI is technological, very important for ethical and social changes. While the world gets closer to achieving AGI, bias, fairness, accountability, job displacement, privacy, and societal impact are some of the issues to deal with squarely. To that respect, enhancing an ethical and inclusive development of AGI will give human upliftment, promote well-being, and social justice.

5.5 Future Perspectives

The development of Artificial General Intelligence is, in the future, both full of enormous potential and also associated with large challenges. AGI holds the very near potential to be able to revolutionize a lot of aspects of our life, such as in the sectors of health, education, industry, and entertainment. It also poses some important questions about how such powerful technology should be managed and integrated into our society.

This illustration depicts the future perspectives of AGI. It includes elements like advanced AI technologies, collaboration between humans and AI, and potential benefits and challenges. It shows futuristic applications in various fields like healthcare, education, and industry.

Figure 5.5: Future Perspectives of AGI

Potential Benefits

AGI can bring a lot of dividends. AGI systems in health could read diagnoses of diseases with higher accuracy and speed as compared to human doctors, saving countless lives in the process. They also could help in developing new treatments and personalizing medicine for different case patients. AGI in education could provide personalized learning-pace and style that meets individual needs-by following up on each student's needs and pace, hence giving quality education to everyone regardless of their place of residence. AGI in industry could work towards the better optimization of business processes, reducing wastage, and enhancing efficiency; hence, costs would be lesser and productivity higher. Driving innovation, it would therefore help to develop new products and services that, as of now, we cannot even imagine. On a daily basis, AGI could release us from day-to-day tasks, enhance creative pursuits, and even offer companionship.

Challenges and Concerns

While this may represent a number of potentially very positive developments, there are also some significant concerns and challenges. One major concern relates to job displacement. That is, in case AGI systems become competent for doing a wide range of things, many jobs may turn out to be effectively automated, thereby creating unemployment and economic inequality. It is important to determine strategies to facilitate such a transition, including aspects such as education and social safety nets. Another major concern is the ethical use of AGI, whereby systems are supposed to ensure a fair, transparent, and accountable society. This will involve taming issues such as biasness in AI algorithms that normally lead to unfair treatment towards certain sets of people. Likelihoods of misuse of AGI for surveillance or autonomous weapons should also be borne in mind.

Governance and Regulation

Proper governance and regulation are essential for both the development and deployment of AGI. It also sets universal standards and frameworks for the responsible development and beneficial use of AGI. The complexity of challenges posed by AGI in many ways requires cooperation between governments, businesses, and the research community. Public engagement in AGI-related issues is similarly important. indeed, there should be enlightenment—through education and information flows—to people about what AGI is, how it works, and what its possible consequences are. There needs to be public input into policy decisions that work on AGI align with societal values and priorities. Contrarily, a balanced approach toward enhancing the development of AGI moves the future a step ahead. Embracing the potentials of AGI must go in tandem with vigorous awareness of the risks and challenges. There is nothing wrong if investment in research and development is pitted against investment in education and other social programs to help people adapt to a rapidly changing world. Another important thing is interdisciplinary collaboration. It is only through such cross-fertilization of insights from computer science and neuroscience with ethicists and social sciences that it could be possible to create AGI agents with intelligence, ethics, and human values.

The promise of AGI, however, lies in being careful, cooperative, and thoughtful while working for its future. We can harness all the power AGI has to offer toward creating a better, more just, and prosperous future for every human being if we work collaboratively and show presence of mind when performing this task.

6

Cognitive Functions and AI Applications

Cognitive functions are mental processes that allow self-performance of tasks ranging from the simplest to the most complex, including perception, attention, memory, decision-making, and problem-solving. These functions are at the root of our ability to comprehend and interact with our surroundings. During the past few decades, breakthroughs in Artificial Intelligence have allowed researchers to replicate many such cognitive functions in machines. It has concretized into the creation of AI systems that are capable of performing tasks earlier considered to be solely performed by human intelligence.

These cognitive functions integrated with AI opened dramatically new opportunities and applications across the board. For example, today AI can already recognize images and read in natural language, perform decisions where large amounts of data might be present. These capabilities are transforming industries—health, finance, education, and so on—to an extent by greatly effective solutions for genuinely complex problems.

In the present chapter, we will review how AI technologies are copying and enhancing human cognitive functions. We will describe how

AI perceives, learns, and decides, and compare this to the human cognitive process. Before describing these mechanisms, it is good to appreciate the tremendous development in AI thus far and the expectation of future development.

6.1 Perception and Sensory Processing

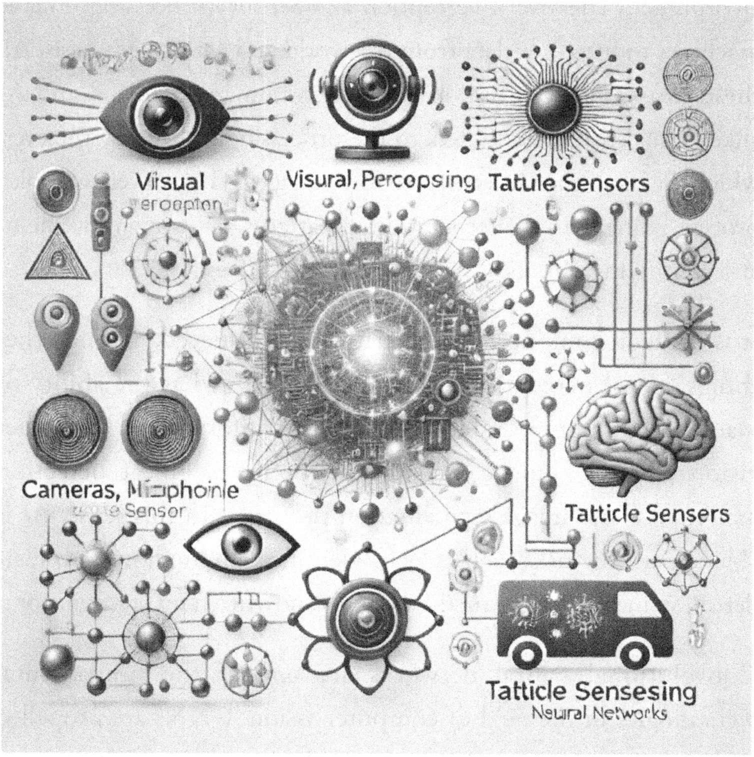

Figure 6.1: illustrates the concept of perception and sensory processing in AI.

It shows how visual, auditory, and tactile data are processed and integrated, with components such as cameras, microphones, and tactile sensors connected to neural networks.

Perception is the means whereby living organisms interpret the environment by organizing sensory information. In humans, perception refers to the integration of information derived from the different sensory inputs, namely, visual, auditory, tactile, gustatory, and olfactory modalities. This allows us to identify objects, understand spatial relation, and hence to interact with our environment effectively. Perception and Sensory Processing: Enable machines to interpret data from the world and act on that basis. All these areas have been well-researched in human cognition and AI alike. Visual perception refers to the processing of light by the eyes, which the brain then interprets to form images. This is a very complex process, going with the recognition of patterns, detecting movement, and identifying objects.

It is through computer vision that AI has achieved, among other things, visual perception, which can be defined as the ability of machines to interpret and understand visual information. Computer vision embraces image recognition methods, object detection techniques, and image segmentation processes. In this sense, AI is able to perform tasks such as facial identification in photos, obstacle detection in self-driving methods, and handwritten text recognition.

Convolutional neural networks are one of the fundamental technologies in the field of computer vision. CNNs are propelled to guard visual information similar to the human brain. In essence, they are interleaved with layers performing convolutions, pooling, and activation functions, which eventually realize the extraction of hierarchical features from images. The very early layers of a CNN might be able to detect edges and textures, while later layers may recognize more complex structures, such as objects and scenes. Different visual perception tasks have been accomplished with state-of-the-art performance using CNNs.

Auditory perception

Auditory perception is the form of processing of sound waves by the ears, which gets interpreted through the brain. Humans use auditory perception to detect sounds and to recognize speech, which interprets groups of words into meaningful expressions usable mainly for communication purposes and interacting with environmental components.

In the case of AI, techniques for auditory perception include speech recognition and natural language processing. Whereas speech recognition can be viewed as a form of translation, it does not seek to translate spoken language as much as turn it into text so that the machines know what the user is commanding. This technology finds its major applications in virtual assistants such as Siri and Alexa, in transcription services, and in voice-activated systems.

Deep learning models, particularly recurrent neural networks and transformers, have been very important tools for this movement toward speech recognition and NLP. The models are able to ingest sequences of data from audio and learn the patterns of speech. For instance, RNNs handle temporal dependencies in an audio signal; thus, they are better at tasks like speech-to-text conversion. On the contrary, transformers apply attention mechanisms to model relevant parts of the input sequence, which greatly helps in accuracy and efficiency for state-of-the-art speech recognition systems.

Tactile Perception

Tactile perception is the sense of touch, that allows humans to feel pressure, temperature, and texture. This sense is essential in tasks such as object manipulation and navigation of environments, as it provides the physical feelings for exploration.

In AI, tactile perception is being researched in connection with robotics, especially when developing robotic hands and grippers. These devices are fitted with sensors, imitating a human's sense of touch. These robots aspire to pick up fragile objects, assemble parts, and even interact with humans.

Tactile sensors in robotics measure forces, pressures, temperatures, and other modalities to provide real-time feedback to the control system. This feedback is considered of central importance as it allows the robot to adjust its behavior on runtime in order to execute tasks precisely and safely. Machine learning algorithms are being used with growing frequency to process such tactile data to better enable the robot's proficiency over a wide variety of objects and tasks.

Multisensory Integration

Multisensory integration is a process by which information from the different sensory modalities is combined into one coherent perception of the environment. In humans, it plays a critical role in navigating the world efficiently because it makes it possible to process visual, auditory, and tactile information simultaneously.

In AI, multisensory integration is such a young field of research being involved in the development of systems that can process and merge data from several sensors. For example, an autonomous vehicle would make use of cameras to get the visual perception, microphones for auditory perception, and LIDAR for tactile perception to the environment in making driving decisions.

This could also foster more robust and accurate perception systems in AI via multisensory integration. In this respect, the AI will be able to reduce uncertainty using complementary or correlated information and also be in a position to detect changes in the environment and respond accordingly. This ability is quite significant, especially in dynamic situations where predictability is low, such as autonomous driving and robotic surgery.

6.2 Attention and Focus

Attention is one of the cognitive processes that deals with focusing on one piece of information at a time while disregarding other sources of information. Attention helps a human being to focus his mind upon relevant things, to filter the distractions, and distribute processing resources optimally within the brain. Attention mechanisms in the case of AI are focused on facilitating machines' ability to recognize information of primary interest for processing and enhance their performance in the task handed to them.

It is showing how self-attention mechanisms in neural networks work. It includes elements such as input sequences, attention weights, and how the model focuses on relevant parts of the input data.

Attention Mechanisms in AI

Attention mechanisms are basically Generic inspirations enunciated from the human ability for focusing on parts of the input while processing information. These mechanisms have made a significant presence in the field of AI, particularly within natural language processing and computer vision.

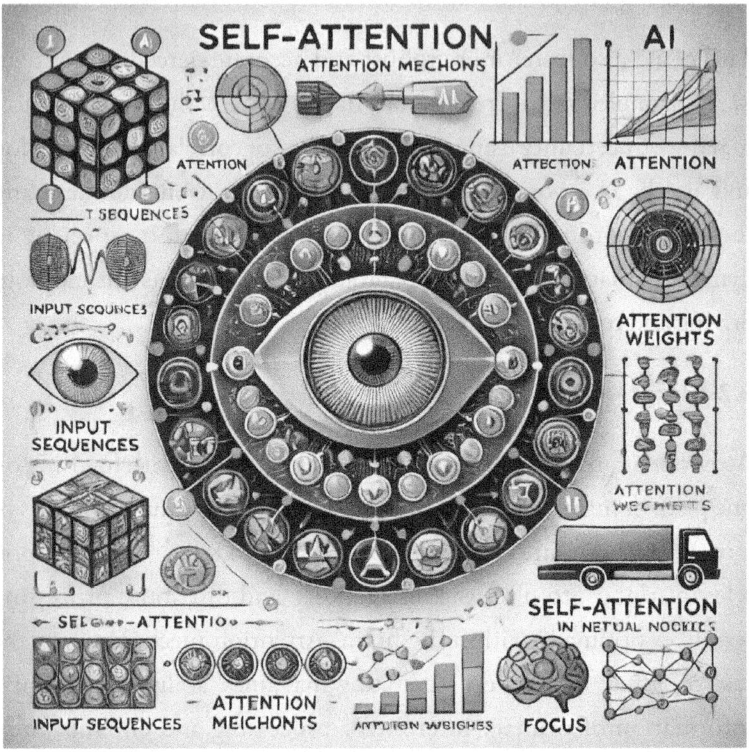

Figure 6.2: illustration depicts attention and focus in AI.

• ***Self-Attention:*** This is an intra-attention mechanism wherein each element of an input sequence attends to all other elements. It allows the model to weigh the relative importance of different parts of the input better and focus on the most relevant information. Self-attention is one of the pivotal building blocks for Transformer architecture, which has swept the field of NLP, allowing models to deal with extremely long-range dependencies and contextual relationships in a text.

• ***Transformers:*** By using self-attention mechanisms, transformers can parallelize the processing of input sequences, unlike traditional RNN EEG. This in return made the architecture result in huge developments in NLP, including models like BERT and GPT-3. With high accuracy, these models perform tasks relating to translation, generation, and question answering.

• ***Attention in Computer Vision:*** Attention models have been applied to computer vision tasks. Attention models applied to the task of image recognition can focus on regions with relevant content, therefore bringing improvements to object detection and classification. For example, the attention-based model, YOLO—You Only Look Once—determines real-time object localization by selective attention on parts of the different inputs.

Attention Mechanism Applications

Attention mechanisms find applications in many AI applications, improving these machines in the handling and trying to make sense of manifold data.

• ***Natural Language Processing:*** In NLP, attention mechanisms are used to enhance performance in machine translation, text summarization, and sentiment analysis. Attention models are able to work out more accurate and coherent translations, summaries, and sentiment predictions by focusing on relevant words and phrases.

• It also allows the model in machine translation to align words in the source language to their corresponding words in the target language. Attention mechanisms Erick et al. support quality translation by ensuring that the translated text gives the proper meaning and context of the original test. The transformer, an attention-based model, set new benchmarks in machine translation, performing better than traditional RNN-based models.

• ***Text Summarization:*** Attention mechanisms are applied to obtain the structure and contextual flow of the sentences and important phrases in a document. This turns attention models into elaborate, very compact getters of rich information for summaries that bear key ideas of the source text.

• ***Sentiment Analysis:*** Attention mechanisms in a model make it 'attentional' to the words and phrases that express emotions and opinions. In this way, the model should be better positioned to correctly predict the sentiment, positive, negative, or neutral, of a given text. Attentional models have been applied in customer review analysis, social media posts, and even survey responses.

• ***Image Captioning:*** Attention mechanisms are applied to image captioning tasks where descriptive captions have to be generated for images. Attention models attend only to relevant regions in the image, generating a more accurate and detailed caption. For example, the Show, Attend, and Tell model uses attention mechanisms to generate a caption by attending to different parts of the image for generating words in the caption.

• ***Speech Recognition:*** Attention mechanisms in speech recognition enable the model to focus on relevant parts of the audio signal and thereby provide an accurate transcription. Attention models are capable of aligning frames of audio with corresponding phonemes or words such that the transcribed text reflects what is actually spoken.

Challenges and Future Directions

Though attention mechanisms have leapfrogged AI systems in many ways, several challenges and future directions still remain.

• ***Scalability:*** That is, attention mechanisms, especially in transformer models, are computationally very expensive and extremely memory-intensive. How to scale these models to more and more extensive datasets and increasingly complicated tasks is part of the ongoing research effort, and researchers are working on techniques like sparse attention and efficient transformers.

• ***Interpretability:*** Knowing how attention mechanisms make decisions is important for constructing transparent and trustworthy AI. This can be done by developing methods for the visualization and interpretation of attention weights so that researchers understand inner mechanisms of models of attention and hence identify potential biases.

• ***Attention-Level Fusion:*** This is a relatively recent area of research, which lies in fusion at the level of attention across multimodalities like text, image, and audio. This implies that, with multimodal attention models, information can be proactively taken from multiple sources and incorporated to enhance performance in tasks that need multi-modal understanding and reasoning.

• Attention mechanisms can be further utilized in human-AI collaborations, where the AI system is expected to focus on task-relevant information, providing useful assistance to humans. For instance, an attention-based recommendation system may get relevant content for users, while an attention model in medical diagnosis may point out those features of interest from a medical image that, actually, hold significant relevance to a clinician.

Attention and focus are the quintessential cognitive features in man and AI systems, governing how efficiently and effectively information is processed. Attention mechanisms basically changed AI into what we know today, more particularly within the areas of NLP and computer vision, performing model. Focus and key into relevant data exclusively. As research in attention mechanisms continues to advance, we can expect further improvements in the capabilities of AI and new applications harnessing the power of attention in solving complex problems.

6.3 Decision Making

Decision making is a preeminent mental process whereby a subject chooses one particular course of action out of a set of available alternatives, characterizing a course of action by available information and desirable outcomes. In humans, decision making is driven by a variety of factors, which include previously acquired experiences, emotions, cognitive biases, and environmental context. One of the most relevant capacities in AI is decision-making, which allows systems to act autonomously to execute tasks independently, adapt to new situations, and optimize outcomes in dynamic environments. This section reviews mechanisms of decision making in AI by drawing parallels with human cognition and real-world applications that harness these AI decision-making capabilities.

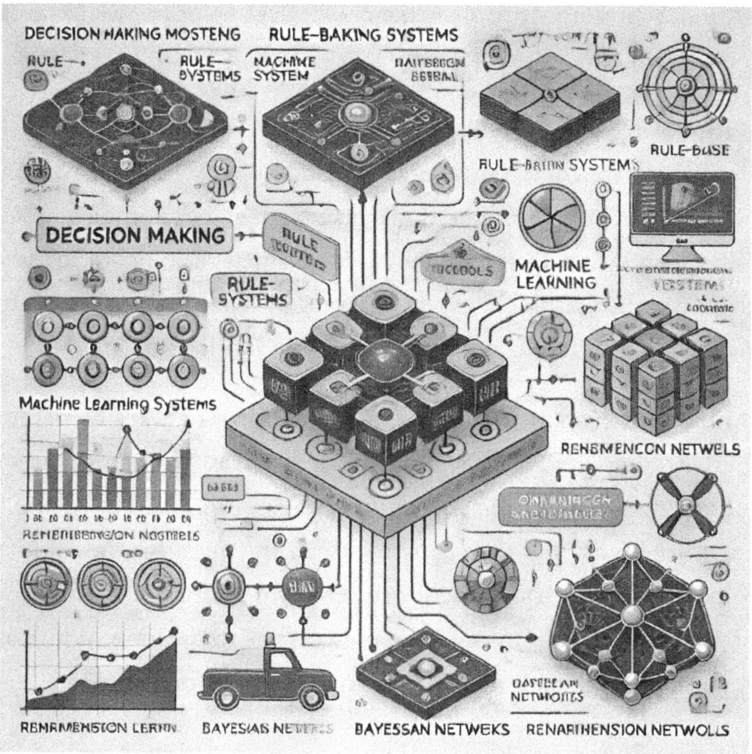

Figure 6.3: illustrates decision making in AI.

It shows various decision-making models such as rule-based systems, machine learning models, reinforcement learning, Bayesian networks, and optimization algorithms, with arrows and labels depicting how data flows through these models to make decisions.

Human Decision Making

Decision making in humans proves to be a highly complex process starring several stages, including perception, interpretation, evaluation, and finally an action. Different models of decision making have been studied by psychologists and neurobiologists in order to understand how people make choices. Some of the well-known models include:

Rational Decision Making: The principle of this model is that alternatives are chosen in a very systematic way to derive maximum utility by an individual. In rational decision making, a problem needs to be defined first, then the alternatives, evaluate the outcome of each alternative, and lastly, choose the best option. This model is, therefore, generally applied in economic and financial decision making.

Bounded Rationality: Bounded rationality was a term coined by Herbert Simon, who defined it as people making decisions that are initially triggered within the confinements of limited information, cognitive limits, and time constraints. In the quest for the optimal solution, there is the tendency to settle for a satisfactory solution or "good enough." This model represents the foundation of human cognition and the role of heuristics in decision making.

Emotional Decision Making: Emotions are a critical ingredient in human decision-making processes. They can affect the ways in which options are perceived and assessed and the motivations to act. For instance, fear might engender cautious behavior, and elation or excitement might embolden risky behavior. If one wants to understand how emotions are intertwined with decision-making processes, then studies in behavioral economics and consumer psychology will be very useful.

Intuitive Decision Making: It involves choices based on gut feelings, instincts, and immediate judgment with not too much deliberation. Such decision-making is mostly fast and unconscious, motorists rely on it to drive through roads with dense traffic. Intuition is best applied where the situation demands speed, such as emergency response and sports.

Decision Making in AI

Decision making in AI is done through various algorithms and models that allow a machine to make an analysis of the data, consider various options, and then choose the best course of action. They can be categorized into several types, each suited to different kinds of decision-making problems.

Rule-Based Systems: In a rule-based system, the decisions are taken based on predefined rules and logic. Here, the conditions are evaluated and an action chosen using if-then statements. The rule-based system is quite simple and easy to implement but sometimes cannot handle a complex and dynamic environment. They find applications in expert systems where domain-specific knowledge is encoded in the form of rules.

Machine Learning Models: In particular, supervised learning models can be trained to make decisions based on the acquisition of patterns from past data. For example, training a machine learning model using labeled training data in classifying emails could result in the model classifying them as spam or otherwise not. Other examples of machine learning algorithms that can be used in decision making include decision trees, random forests, and support vector machines.

Reinforcement Learning: It is that type of machine learning wherein an agent learns from its interaction with the environment itself and feedback in the form of rewards or penalties. As a result, the agent would learn the policy for maximizing the total rewards at the end. This will be the best solution for sequential decision-making problems like playing video games, robotic control, and autonomous driving. Popular algorithms range from Q-learning to deep Q-networks applied for various types of applications involving RL.

Bayesian Networks: Bayesian networks are probabilistic graphical models of variables and their conditional or causal dependencies. Such networks can be used to compute the probabilities of different outcomes against observed data in a scenario, thereby allowing decision making. Bayesian networks are useful in situations where uncertainty and incomplete information exist—for example, in medical diagnosis and risk assessment.

Optimization Algorithms: The objective of an optimization algorithm is to optimize the solution space for an optimum solution, either by maximizing or minimizing an objective function. Some examples of optimization techniques applied in decision making are Linear Programming, Genetic Algorithms, and Particle Swarm Optimization. Such areas of application may emanate from resource allocations, scheduling, and logistics.

Applications of AI in Decision Making

AI-driven decision making finds its application in various industries, mainly increasing efficiency, accuracy, and productivity. Some of the principal applications are:

It is applied in healthcare through AI systems, which assists in clinical decision-making processes. For instance, AI algorithms analyze medical images to detect opportunistic diseases such as cancer and predict patient outcomes against their electronic health records. Extraction Support AI-driven decision support systems help clinicians make informed decisions to improve patient care by decreasing medical errors.

Finance: in the financial sector, AI is applied in algorithmic trading, risk management, and fraud detection. When it comes to investment strategy, AI algorithms analyze market data and execute trades at lightning speeds for optimal returns. In the case of risk management, credit risks are assessed, fraudulent transactions flagged off, and compliance with the provisions of regulatory laws ensured. AI-driven decision-making enhances operational efficiency and security related to financial operations.

Manufacturing: The manufacturing process is optimized by means of better production planning, quality control, and predictive maintenance. Algorithms analyze the sensor data of the equipment used in the manufacturing process to predict failures and conduct maintenance checks in view of decreasing downtimes and related costs. Quality control makes use of AI systems that inspect for flaws in a product and that standards of manufacture are observed. In this regard, AI-driven decision making improves both efficiency and reliability in manufacturing.

Supply Chain Management: AI decision making within the domain of supply chain management applies to several subjects, including inventory management, demand forecasting, and logistics optimization. The algorithms of artificial intelligence study historical sales data and other factors external to the business for demand estimation in order to maintain optimal inventory levels and to prevent or reduce stockouts. This ensures timely and inexpensive delivery through AI-driven route optimization in logistics. AI drives supply chains to be more nimble and responsive.

Autonomous Vehicles: AVs use AI to make decisions in real-time within dynamic and uncertain environments. The AI algorithms process data from sensors, cameras, and LIDAR to perceive surroundings and recognize obstacles in their path and make driving decisions; autonomous vehicles with reinforcement learning and deep learning models execute navigation via difficult traffic conditions, optimize routes, and ensure safety for passengers. AI-driven decision making is the key to developing and deploying self-driving cars.

Customer Service: AI-based chatbots and virtual assistants continuously improve customer service by rendering real-time responses to customers' queries and saving them from hassle. Systems that can emulate the processing of natural language, through machine learning, understand the questions of customers, retrieve relevant information, and formulate apt replies. AI-driven decision-making in customer service helps increase efficiency, reduces response time, and improves customer satisfaction.

Energy Management: AI optimizes energy management by analyzing the consumption patterns, predicting demand, and controlling energy distribution. AI algorithms in smart grids linearize the balance of supply and demand, creating an efficient usage and having reduced wastage of energy. AI-driven decision making in energy management supports sustainability and reduces operational costs.

6.4 Emotion and AI

Emotions are central in the human perception: they dictate decision, perceive the world and define social interactions; they hold the key to welfare. A challenging and exciting frontier for the development of intelligent systems is thus represented by the possibility of understanding them and mimicking emotional processes. Putting emotion into AI will mean to create not only a machine able to do but also interact with humans in a more natural, empathetic, and effective way. This paper discusses issues associated with the importance of emotions in AI, simulation of emotional manifestations, and practical applications and gives rise to a number of ethical concerns for emotion-aware AI.

Emotions are an integral part of the mental activity of human beings. They help in filtering information and concentrating on relevant information, guiding one while making decisions regarding social interaction. Emotions can enhance learning, improve problem-solving abilities, and motivate behavior. For example, fear may trigger a fleeing or fighting response, whereas happiness may increase positive behaviors. Emotions also play a very significant role in communication because they enable a person to express his or her emotions and perceive those of other people both verbally and nonverbally.

It is showing how AI recognizes and simulates emotions through facial expression analysis, speech emotion recognition, and physiological signal analysis. It includes elements like neural networks and emotion-driven behaviors in robots and virtual agents.

There are several approaches and technologies for creating AI systems able to recognize, interpret, and simulate emotions. Affective computing, sometimes also called emotion AI, would try to bridge the emotional chasm between man's emotional experiences and the machine's responses. Emotion recognition forms the very first step towards developing emotion-aware AI. Various inputs, including facial expressions, voice tones, and body language, as well as physiological signals, represent the ways in which human feelings are detected and interpreted in this paper.

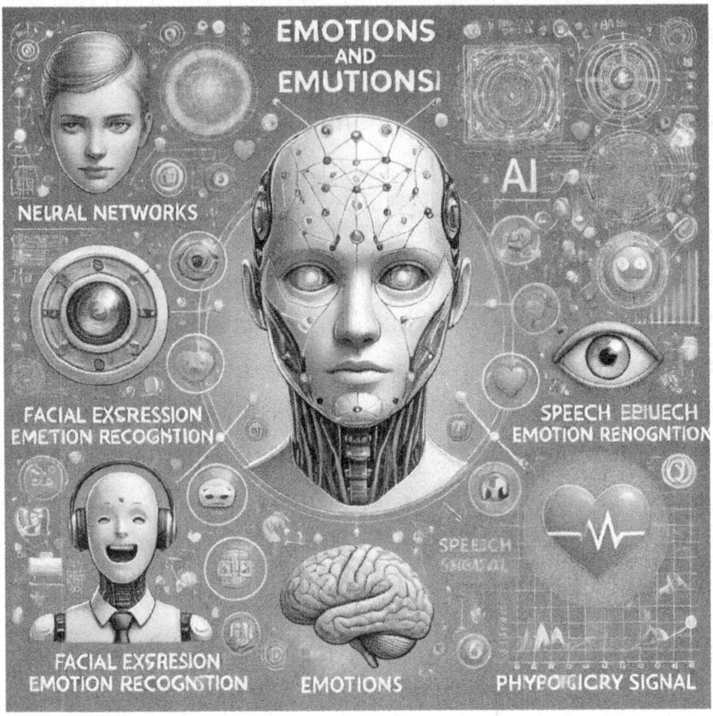

Figure 6.4: illustration depicts emotions and AI

Emotion recognition can be achieved with methodologies such as facial expression analysis, speech emotion recognition, and physiological signal analysis. AI algorithms analyze facial features and movements by applying Convolutional Neural Networks to extract characteristics that could correspond to different emotional states in images and videos.

This includes speech emotion recognition, which is realized through pitch, tone of voice, and rhythm for the determination of emotional expressions using machine learning models like recurrent neural networks and transformers that process audio data in regard to emotional nuances in speech. The analysis of physiological signals measures physiologic responses with devices that record heart rate, skin conductance, and brain activity, among others, which gives a supplementary set of data points that may infer emotional states.

Beyond detection, AI systems can also be constructed to act emotionately. This can include behavior disorderliness, expression, and verbal responses that give an impression of a certain emotion. Affective dialogue systems engage in emotionally conscious conversations about the setting. It understands user feelings and responds accordingly to their needs in order to create more enjoyable and supportive interactions. For example, a virtual therapist might use some of the empathetic responses to help users manage their emotions. It is possible to program robots and virtual agents for behaviors that reflect emotional states, such as a "sad" robot moving slowly and averting eye contact or a "happy" robot through animated movements and cheerful expressions.

In the majority of cases, efficient reproduction of emotion occurs in AI systems through models inspired by psychological theories of emotions. Some of the common models are the Basic Emotions Model, the Dimensional Model, and Appraisal Theory. Psychologist Paul Ekman's Basic Emotions Model includes the classification of basic emotions into six categories: happiness, sadness, fear, disgust, anger, and surprise. In this framework, AI systems are trained to recognize and imitate basic emotions. The Dimensional Model depicts emotions in a two-dimensional space along two axes—the valence axis from positive to negative and the arousal axis from calm to excited—thereby representing emotions in a much more multi-dimensional way. According to appraisal theory, emotions are a result of cognitive appraisals of events. AI systems can then simulate emotions by the assessment of a situation against criteria like relevance, goal congruence, and coping potential.

Emotionally aware AI finds many applications across different domains in enhancing human-machine interaction and insight into human behavior. In health care, it can contribute to mental health by providing POC with therapy and emotional support. AI-driven chatbots and virtual therapists can provide empathetic conversations, monitor emotional well-being, and advice techniques to cope up with stress, anxiety, or depression in individuals. Such systems shall monitor early warning signs of emotional distress and provide recommendations for suitable interventions. Emotion-aware AI in customer service can make for comprehensive overhauls in user experience by identifying and acting on customer emotions. In this way, virtual assistants and chatbots can pick up frustration or dissatisfaction from the voice or text of customers and make their responses as useful and supporting as possible to improve customer satisfaction and loyalty.

In education, emotion-aware AI can make the learning experiences of students move along based on his/her emotional state. For example, if an intelligent tutoring system could recognize a frustrated student and encourage him or make things easier to keep him engaged, it would create a more inviting atmosphere for learning. Emotion-aware AI, in the entertainment sector, would enhance the experience of video games and virtual reality. Games may change the storyline, hardness levels, and activities to make gamers always play and have fun by reading gamers' feelings. Emotion-aware robots can provide companionship and assistance in caregiving support for special needs by interacting with humans in a natural and efficient way. Such robots can help in social interactions by responding emotionally, as humans do, intuitively and emphatically. Similarly, emotion-attuned AI can be applied in marketing and advertising to analyze the consumers' emotions for making a suitable marketing strategy and preparing an effective advertisement. Knowing the feel of customers about products and brands will help a company have a more personalized and thus effective marketing campaign. It can also be used in understanding the impact evoked by an advertisement on audiences' minds and fine-tune its content accordingly.

While putting emotions into AI reaps numerous benefits, important ethical issues stated herein must be brought to the forefront and answered. Emotion-sensing usually involves the collection and analysis of sensitive personal data. Thus, ensuring that people provide informed consent and protecting privacy is very important. AI systems have to treat emotion-related data in a responsible manner and comply with data protection regulations. Emotion recognition algorithms can be biased, and hence estimate emotions either inaccurately or unfairly. For example, cultural differences within emotional expression lead to misinterpretation. The development and validation of emotion recognition systems should thus be based on different populations in order to ensure fairness and accuracy. Emotion-aware AI can manipulate human feelings: an ethical problem. For example, emotional insights could be used to manipulate consumer behavior and political opinions, hence opening the door for abuses of autonomy and trust. In case individuals are to have trust maintained and ethical acceptability, it is important to have transparency on how their emotional data are being used and what emotion-aware interactions are for. There could be a situation whereby over-reliance on emotion-aware AI as a means for support leads to human contact being reduced and social isolation ensuing. AI systems must be designed in a manner that, as much as possible, they enhance, rather than replace, human relationships and support networks.

6.5 Creativity and Innovation

Creativity and innovation are often regarded as distinctly human traits, driving art, science, technology, and culture forward. These capabilities allow humans to generate new ideas, solve complex problems, and adapt to changing environments. With the advent of advanced artificial intelligence (AI), there is growing interest in understanding how AI can replicate or even augment these creative processes. This section explores the relationship between AI and human creativity, the mechanisms that enable AI to exhibit creative behavior, and the implications of AI-driven innovation across various fields.

It is showing the use of generative models like GANs, neural networks, and evolutionary algorithms. It includes examples such as AI-generated art, music, and designs, and how these models generate novel and valuable ideas.

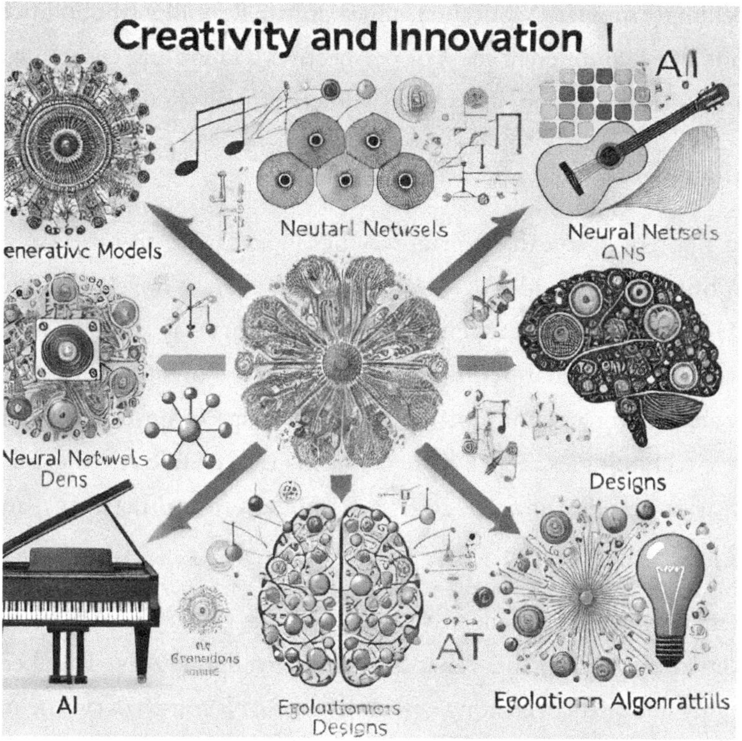

Figure 6.5: illustrates creativity and innovation in AI

Understanding Creativity and Innovation

Creativity involves generating ideas that are both novel and valuable. It encompasses a wide range of activities, from artistic expression and scientific discovery to problem-solving and invention. Innovation, on the other hand, refers to the implementation of creative ideas in a way that adds value, often resulting in new products, services, or processes.

In humans, creativity is influenced by cognitive processes such as divergent thinking (the ability to generate multiple solutions to a problem), convergent thinking (the ability to find the best solution), associative thinking (making connections between seemingly unrelated concepts), and cognitive flexibility (the ability to shift between different ideas or perspectives). Emotions, experiences, and social interactions also play a significant role in fostering creativity.

AI and Creativity

AI's potential to exhibit creativity lies in its ability to process vast amounts of data, identify patterns, and generate novel solutions. Machine learning, particularly deep learning, has enabled AI to perform tasks that require a certain degree of creativity, such as generating art, composing music, writing, and even inventing new technologies. The key mechanisms that enable AI to exhibit creative behavior include generative models, neural networks, and evolutionary algorithms.

Generative Models: Generative models, such as Generative Adversarial Networks (GANs) and Variational Autoencoders (VAEs), have been highly successful in creating new content. GANs consist of two neural networks—a generator and a discriminator—that work together to produce realistic images, music, or text. The generator creates new data, while the discriminator evaluates its authenticity, guiding the generator to improve its outputs over time. VAEs, on the other hand, encode input data into a lower-dimensional space and then decode it back, allowing the generation of new, similar data. These models have been used to create everything from realistic human faces to novel pieces of art.

Neural Networks: Neural networks, especially deep neural networks, are capable of learning complex patterns and relationships within data. They have been used to compose music, generate text, and even create visual art. For example, AI models like Open AI's GPT-3 can write essays, stories, and poems by learning from vast amounts of text data. Similarly, deep learning algorithms can analyze musical compositions and create new pieces in the style of famous composers.

Evolutionary Algorithms: Inspired by the process of natural selection, evolutionary algorithms generate solutions to problems by iteratively selecting and combining the best-performing candidates. These algorithms have been used in design optimization, where they evolve novel solutions that might not be immediately apparent to human designers. For example, evolutionary algorithms can generate innovative architectural designs or optimize engineering components for better performance.

Applications of AI-Driven Creativity

AI-driven creativity has numerous applications across various fields, enhancing human creativity and driving innovation in ways that were previously unimaginable.

Art and Entertainment: In the art world, AI is being used to create original paintings, music, and literature. AI-generated art has gained popularity, with some pieces being exhibited in galleries and sold at auctions. AI musicians can compose music that rivals human composers, while AI writers can produce poems, stories, and scripts. These creative outputs are not only valuable in their own right but also inspire human artists to explore new creative avenues.

Design and Architecture: AI is transforming design and architecture by offering new tools for creativity and innovation. Generative design algorithms can produce a wide range of design options based on specific parameters, allowing architects and designers to explore innovative solutions. AI can also optimize designs for functionality, aesthetics, and sustainability, leading to more efficient and innovative structures.

Scientific Research: In scientific research, AI is accelerating the pace of discovery by generating hypotheses, designing experiments, and analyzing data. AI algorithms can identify patterns in complex datasets, leading to new insights and breakthroughs. For example, AI has been used to discover new materials, predict protein structures, and even generate potential drug candidates. By augmenting human creativity, AI is driving innovation in fields such as chemistry, biology, and physics.

Business and Marketing: In the business world, AI is being used to develop innovative products and marketing strategies. AI can analyze consumer data to identify trends and preferences, guiding the development of new products that meet market demands. In marketing, AI-driven content generation and personalized advertising are enhancing customer engagement and driving sales. AI's ability to analyze vast amounts of data and generate creative solutions is transforming the way businesses operate and compete.

Education and Training: AI is also making strides in education by creating personalized learning experiences and innovative educational tools. AI-driven platforms can adapt to individual learning styles and provide customized content, enhancing the learning process. Additionally, AI can generate interactive simulations and virtual environments that offer immersive and engaging learning experiences. By fostering creativity and innovation in education, AI is preparing students for the challenges of the future.

Creativity and innovation are the most important and integral drivers of development in art, science, technology, and culture. Now, AI can emulate such creative processes and provide new tools and powers to boost human creativity. Knowing how AI can demonstrate creative behavior, as well as the potential fields of application in very diversified domains, will help leverage the strength of AI-powered creativity for driving innovation and solving complex problems. There is also the side of the ethical considerations that must be followed on how AI-generated creativity is used in a responsible and inclusive way. With the possibility of exploration in the future at the intersection of AI and creativity, we can look forward to times when intelligent systems work together with humans in services pushing the boundaries of the possible.

7
Challenges and Future Directions

We are on the threshold of an AI_CONSTANT-driven new era, and if effectively harnessed, the transformational potential of it across every nook and cranny of our lives is mammoth. Again, all these very promises come bundled with an array of challenges that need to be responded to in trying responsibly to manage AI's full potential. The chapter discusses challenges to overcome in widespread adoption, but also conjectures on future directions, which will have an impact on the course of development of AI. AI has already made big strides in all areas running from healthcare, finance, and education to entertainment. The following critical issues are supposed to be taken seriously. These vary from technical issues associated with data quality and algorithms that can be biased to ethical concerns related to privacy, fairness, accountability, job displacement, and economic inequality, after the integration of AI in society, but also another challenge is the establishment of new regulatory frameworks. Moreover, with the increase in the level of autonomy, AI systems would become very important in terms of safety and reliability. There lies a risk of unintended consequences and a danger of malicious use of AI technology. In this regard, robust, transparent, and secure AI would be essential for gaining public trust and ensuring benefits to humankind as a whole. The future of AI itself is full of prospects. Machine learning, natural language processing, and robotics will continue to stretch the potentials for application of AI. In that light, collaborative work between researchers, people involved in policy formulation, and heads of industry will be very necessary to start off and drive AI development along lines consistent with the values and priorities of society.

The chapter has views on some of the important challenges that AI faces today and points out some possible solutions and future directions. If these challenges are faced head-on, and an environment of innovation and ethical responsibility is fostered, then the path AI takes can be directed in the right way, to leave a positive mark on our world, increasing our potential capability to enabling a life with values added to it.

7.1 Technical Problems

As AI continues to develop and integrate into many walks of life, there will be a stream of challenging technical problems involved that need to be attended to if AI is to be deployed safely, effectively, and equitably. These are spread out across a wide spectrum: data quality, algorithmic bias, interpretability, scalability, computational resources, and security. Understanding and answering these technical challenges is significant for continued progress and the responsible use of AI.

It is including data quality, algorithmic bias, interpretability, scalability, computational resources, and security. Each challenge is represented by an icon and label, providing a visual overview of the complexities involved in AI development.

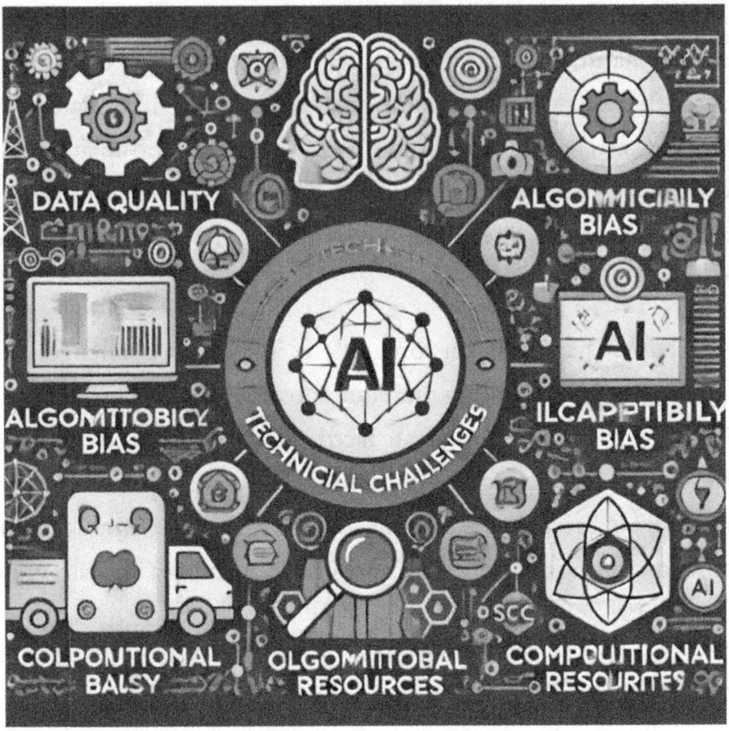

Figure 7.1: illustrates various technical challenges in AI.

Data Quality and Availability

This is one of the most technically challenging areas in AI: ensuring data of good quality and, correspondingly, its availability. Put differently, skewed words for data are core to the AI systems. Why? Because the performance of this system is highly dependent on the quality of the data used to train these models. The poor quality data will birth inaccurate models, while lack thereof may limit developing robust AI systems.

Data Collection: To train effective AI models, representative and diverse high-quality data needs to be collected. Inherent in such data collection efforts, however, may be challenges with privacy, restrictive clauses involving intellectual property, or sometimes simply a question of logistics. More importantly, data diversity has to be ensured to avoid biases created from the homogeneity of the dataset.

Data Cleaning and Preprocessing: Raw data contains a lot of noise, errors, and inconsistencies that may impact model performance. The process of detection and correction of such issues in the data cleaning and preprocessing stage is time-consuming and expertise-intensive. Among many others, imputation, normalization, and outlier detection techniques are applied to prepare data for training.

Labeling and Annotation: Most of the supervised learning tasks require labeled data. Labeling of large datasets is time-consuming and expensive. Moreover, incomplete or inconsistent labeling results in poor performance by models. This has made semi-supervised and unsupervised learning techniques that work with limited labeled data an active area of research to mitigate this challenge.

7.2 Ethical Considerations

Artificial intelligence (AI), while fast turning into an ever more indispensable component of life, has managed to create some very serious ethical considerations which are associated with its deployment. These considerations include fairness, transparency, accountability, privacy, and other societal impacts. Next, these dimensions are presented in particulars, together with their implications and how they should be navigated.

Figure 7.2: highlights ethical considerations in AI

It is including fairness, transparency, accountability, privacy, and societal impact. Each concept is represented by an icon and label, providing a clear overview of the ethical dimensions involved in AI.

Fairness in AI should be observed to ensure that systems are not perpetuating or causing more biased outcomes or inequalities. Since AI models are trained based on data, they tend to pick up prejudices from society, which are embedded in the training data. For example, biased historic data about hiring can be a reason for discriminative AI-driven hiring practices. What's more, ensuring fairness would mean using diverse, representative, and unbiased training data.

Mechanisms for detecting and mitigating bias within algorithms will be another very important addition. Due to that, these models have to be audited regularly for possible outcomes that might be discriminatory.

In this regard, transparency and explain ability become very critical, more so in areas as important as health, finances, and criminal justice. Most advanced models, particularly deep learning ones, are inherently "black boxes"; that is, it is pretty difficult to know how they really go about their decision-making. One approach toward enhancing transparency in AI involves developing interpretable models and applying techniques like Explainable AI to get clear explanations of the predictions. This not only contributes to the building of trust but also enhances regulatory compliance and ethical accountability.

The more autonomous AI systems become, the more complex the issue of accountability. Accountability for actions and decisions of AI is therefore of fundamental importance from an ethical and legal point of view. To this end, strong legal frameworks have to be drafted, as well as effective dissimilation of roles and liabilities among the stakeholders in AI development. Ethical guidelines, control structures, and independent review boards or regulatory bodies should oversee the conformance of AI systems with those standards. Coupled with this would be the requirement for privacy and data protection. Most AI systems are powered by vast datasets, usually containing personal information. In that case, guaranteeing data privacy would require techniques such as differential privacy, which adds noise to the dataset and helps protect the individual data, and federated learning, whereby model training happens across several devices without actually sharing the raw data. Clear communication about data policies and practices is very important in building trust and making sure that privacy rights are respected. The societal impact of AI extends beyond the individual ethical issues to broader implications on structures of society and human relationships. Amongst these in the taster catalogue of greater concerns are disruptions to job activities and economic effects. Surely, AI will be able to drive economic growth, but at the risk it will disenfranchise certain jobs, hence their holders, jobless. These impacts shall be addressed through policies such as transition programs for workers, retraining, and others aimed at cushioning those affected by job displacement.

Public engagement in AI is thus highly important for dealing with its ethical and social implications. Engaging a plethora of stakeholders—from policymakers all the way down to technologists, ethicists, and public citizens—underwrites that the multiplicity of views are inducted into the AI development process. Due to open and socially responsive communication about benefits and risks of AI, it sends a strong wave of gaining public trust and collaboration. Ethics in AI must be educated and literate if it is going to understand the implications of AI and make informed choices. Artificial intelligence ethics can be infused into education and training; it will promote the capacity needed with a strong ethical foundation for future technologists and decision-makers. Encouraging interdisciplinary education that marries technical skills with ethical and social understanding will nurture a culture of ethical awareness.

The attention to ethical considerations of AI demands collective actions on the part of researchers, developers, decision-makers, and civil society. Understanding and grappling with these challenges will pave the way for the responsible development and deployment of AI systems that are fair, transparent, accountable, and beneficial to society.

7.3 Regulation and Governance

With the rapid growth in AI technologies, there is an important call for robust regulatory and governance frameworks to ensure that their development and use are ethical and safe. The regulation and governance of AI involve creating policies, standards, and oversight mechanisms that answer questions related to safety, fairness, transparency, accountability, and ethical use.

Figure 7.3: depicts regulation and governance of AI

It is showing elements such as legal frameworks, industry standards, oversight mechanisms, and international cooperation. Each aspect is represented by an icon and label, providing a clear visual representation of the regulatory landscape.

Effective regulation begins with comprehensive legal frameworks that set out roles, responsibilities, and liabilities of the stakeholders in AI. These frameworks need to deal with data privacy, security, bias, and accountability. To do so, policymakers will have to work closely with technologists, ethicists, legal experts, and industry stakeholders on regulations that balance innovation with public safety and ethical considerations. Traditional regulatory mechanisms may not match the dynamism of AI very well. A much more flexible outcome-based or principles-based approach to regulation would emphasize the attainment of certain ends—fairness, safety, and others—that imbue it with elasticity necessary for more adaptive and responsive regulation.

Development of industry-specific standards and guidelines assures the safe and ethical applications of AI in various sectors. That is, standard-setting bodies like ISO and IEEE are very instrumental in the development and promotion of standards. Independent oversight structures oversee adherence to regulations and ethical standards. That kind of continuous assessment is provided by such independent structures of oversight as ethics committees focused on AI, review boards, and regulating agencies. Transparency processes of oversight instill confidence with the general public and ensure accountability. Effective governance of AI will require public engagement and stakeholder participation. Policymakers and regulatory bodies have to engage a variety of stakeholders in the development of inclusive regulations. Public consultations, workshops, and an advisory council create meaningful dialogue and collaboration so that governance frameworks encompass a diversity of perspectives. It is a fact that the global challenges created by AI and the requirements for harmonized regulatory frameworks will be solved through international cooperation. At this level, multilateral organizations with leading roles in the United Nations and the Organisation for Economic Co-operation and Development become very important regarding international cooperation on artificial intelligence governance. The ethical dimension should lie at the heart of AI regulation and governance; ethical considerations of fairness, transparency, accountability, or respect for human rights should be enshrined in regulatory frameworks. Ethical guidelines and behavioral codes set the basis for responsible development and the usage of AI.

No different from self-driving cars and drones, autonomous systems are notoriously difficult to govern. Their safety, reliability, and ethical behavior can only be guaranteed by specialized frameworks that answer characteristics and risks of a safety standard, certification process, and liability framework.

AI governance should also take into account AI ethics, to be instilled at the very beginning with ethical impact assessments and review procedures. Funding agencies and institutions are enjoined to make ethics considerations of research proposals in AI the rule.

7.4 Interdisciplinary Collaboration

Interdisciplinary collaboration is vital for addressing AI's multifaceted challenges and harnessing its full potential. AI's complexity and broad impact necessitate integrating diverse perspectives from various disciplines, including computer science, engineering, ethics, law, social sciences, and humanities.

AI development and deployment involve technical, ethical, social, and legal considerations that cannot be adequately addressed by any single discipline. Interdisciplinary collaboration fosters a holistic understanding of AI's impact and innovative solutions informed by multiple perspectives. For example, while computer scientists and engineers focus on technical aspects, ethicists and social scientists provide insights into ethical and societal implications, ensuring responsible design and deployment.

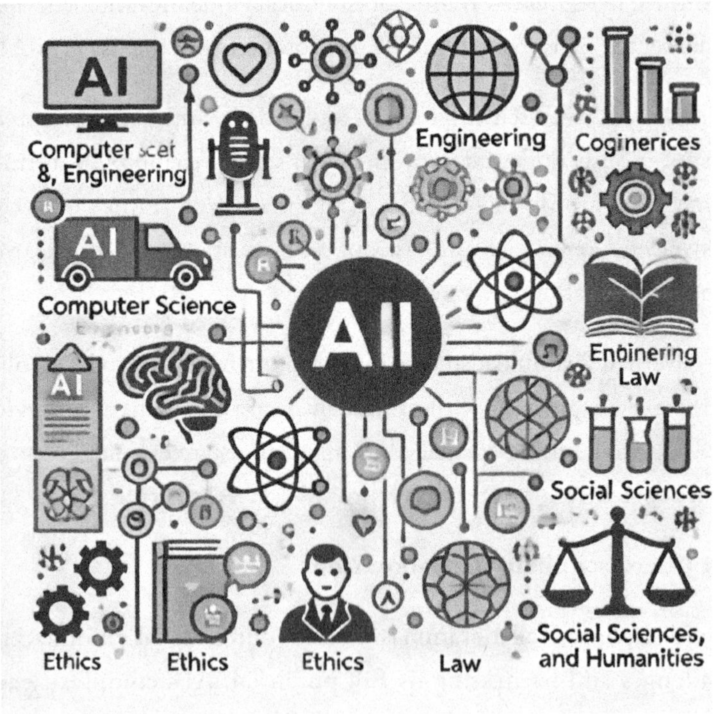

Figure 7.4: illustrates interdisciplinary collaboration in AI

It is showing interactions between fields such as computer science, engineering, ethics, law, social sciences, and humanities. Each discipline and their connections are represented by icons and labels, providing a clear overview of the collaborative landscape.

One key benefit of interdisciplinary collaboration is identifying and addressing ethical issues early in AI development. Ethicists can conduct ethical impact assessments, identify potential biases, and develop mitigation strategies. Legal experts provide guidance on regulatory compliance and navigating legal landscapes. Social scientists study AI's societal impact and ensure alignment with societal values and needs.

Interdisciplinary collaboration also fosters innovation by combining diverse skill sets and knowledge bases. Different disciplines offer unique problem-solving approaches, leading to novel solutions that might not emerge within a single field. For instance, collaboration between AI researchers and neuroscientists advances understanding and replication of human cognitive processes, while partnerships between AI developers and healthcare professionals drive medical diagnostics and treatment innovations.

Fostering effective interdisciplinary collaboration requires creating environments that encourage open communication, mutual respect, and shared goals. Academic institutions, research organizations, and industry should promote interdisciplinary research initiatives and provide collaboration platforms. This includes interdisciplinary research centers, joint funding programs, and collaborative projects.

Education and training play crucial roles in promoting interdisciplinary collaboration. Integrating interdisciplinary courses and programs into curricula equips students with knowledge and skills to work across disciplines. Offering joint programs in AI and ethics or AI and law prepares students to navigate complex ethical and legal issues. Encouraging interdisciplinary research opportunities provides practical experience in collaborative work.

Collaborative networks and partnerships facilitate interdisciplinary engagement. Establishing networks that connect researchers, practitioners, and stakeholders from different disciplines fosters knowledge exchange and collaboration. Forums and conferences bringing together AI researchers, ethicists, legal experts, and policymakers provide platforms for discussing ethical and societal implications and developing collaborative solutions.

Funding agencies and research institutions support interdisciplinary collaboration by prioritizing and funding interdisciplinary research projects. Providing funding for interdisciplinary initiatives incentivizes researchers to engage in collaborative work and address complex challenges from multiple perspectives. Funding programs requiring interdisciplinary teams or promoting cross-disciplinary collaboration help bridge gaps between fields and drive innovation.

Industry partnerships play significant roles in fostering interdisciplinary collaboration. Collaboration between academia and industry leads to practical solutions addressing real-world challenges. Partnerships between AI companies and healthcare providers drive advancements in medical AI applications, while collaborations between AI developers and legal firms address regulatory and ethical challenges.

7.5 Future Perspectives

As we look to the future, AI is poised to transform various aspects of society profoundly. Understanding these future perspectives is essential for preparing for AI's continued evolution and ensuring its development aligns with societal goals and values.

One promising direction for AI is the development of artificial general intelligence (AGI), which refers to highly autonomous systems capable of outperforming humans in most economically valuable work. AGI has the potential to revolutionize industries, drive technological advancements, and address complex global challenges. However, AGI development raises significant ethical and societal concerns, including control, safety, and unintended consequences. Ensuring AGI development is guided by ethical principles and robust safety measures is crucial to prevent harm and ensure AGI benefits humanity.

Integrating AI with emerging technologies, such as quantum computing, biotechnology, and the Internet of Things (IoT), is another key future direction. Quantum computing can revolutionize AI by enabling vast data processing at unprecedented speeds, leading to breakthroughs in drug discovery, climate modeling, and optimization problems. AI and biotechnology convergence promises advancements in personalized medicine, genomics, and bioinformatics. AI and IoT integration enhances smart cities, autonomous vehicles, and industrial automation, driving efficiency and innovation.

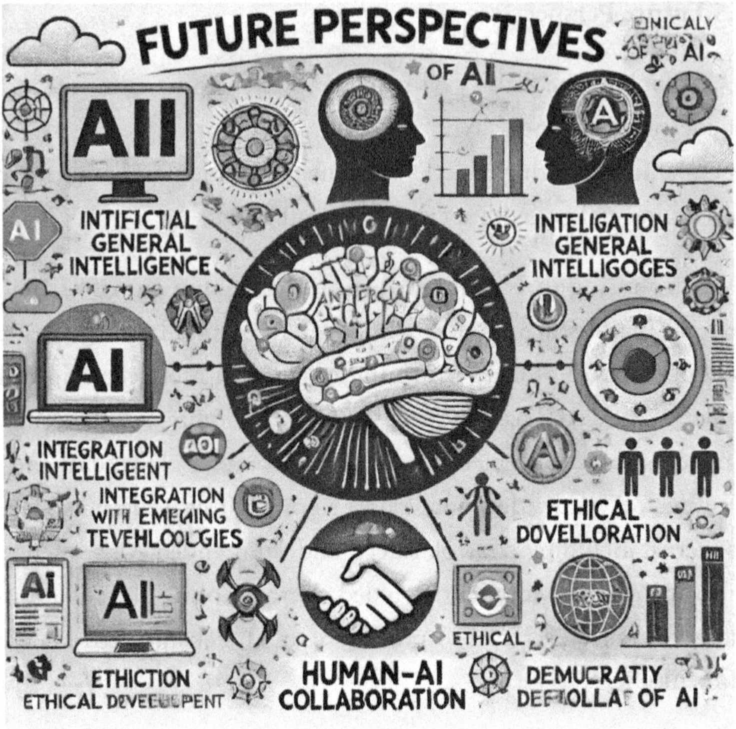

Figure 7.5: depicts future perspectives in AI

It is highlighting concepts such as AGI (artificial general intelligence), integration with emerging technologies, ethical development, human-AI collaboration, and democratization of AI. Each concept is represented by an icon and label, providing a visual summary of the future directions of AI.

Ethical considerations and responsible AI development remain central to AI's future. As AI technologies become more pervasive, ensuring their development and use align with societal values and respect human rights is essential. Addressing fairness, transparency, accountability, and privacy is crucial for maintaining public trust. Developing ethical guidelines, regulatory frameworks, and oversight mechanisms is vital for navigating AI's ethical landscape and ensuring responsible use.

Human-AI collaboration is another important future perspective. AI has the potential to augment human capabilities and enhance productivity. Designing AI systems that complement human skills, provide meaningful assistance, and respect human autonomy is essential for creating positive and productive human-AI interactions. Collaborative AI, where humans and AI systems work together to achieve common goals, can drive innovation and improve decision-making across various fields, from healthcare and education to business and public administration.

Democratizing AI involves making AI technologies accessible to a broader range of users, including small and medium-sized enterprises (SMEs), individual developers, and non-technical users. Developing user-friendly AI tools, platforms, and frameworks lowers barriers to entry. Democratizing AI fosters innovation, drives economic growth, and ensures AI benefits are widely shared.

Education and workforce development are critical for preparing for AI's future. As AI technologies evolve, demand for skills in AI development, deployment, and management will grow. Integrating AI education into curricula, providing training and upskilling opportunities, and promoting lifelong learning are essential for building an AI-ready workforce. Encouraging interdisciplinary education that combines technical skills with ethical, legal, and social understanding is crucial for developing well-rounded AI professionals.

Addressing global challenges and promoting sustainable development are also key future perspectives. AI has the potential to contribute to solving pressing issues like climate change, public health, and poverty. Leveraging AI for social good can develop solutions that improve environmental sustainability, enhance healthcare delivery, and promote economic and social inclusion. Collaborative efforts between governments, industry, academia, and civil society are essential for harnessing AI's power to address global challenges and promote sustainable development.

In conclusion, AI's future perspectives are filled with opportunities and challenges that will shape its development and societal impact. Understanding and preparing for AI's continued evolution ensures its development aligns with societal goals and values, driving innovation and improving human well-being. By addressing ethical considerations, fostering interdisciplinary collaboration, and promoting education and workforce development, we can navigate AI's complexities and unlock its full potential for the benefit of society.

Conclusion

Inspired by our examination of the intricate interplay between neuroscience and artificial intelligence, one thing is clear: the similarities between the human brain and AI, genuinely fascinating, carry a profound impact by themselves. In this book, we have gone through a journey from the very basics, starting with neurons and neural networks, to advanced concepts like consciousness and Artificial General Intelligence, the enormous potential, and challenges lying ahead.

Knowing the neural network architecture and pattern of connectivity not only yields valuable lessons into how we could build more powerfully efficient AI, but also drawing analogies between biological processes, such as learning and memory, and their artificial counterparts, we have focused on how AI can learn, adapt, and evolve. Cognitive functions and applications are discussed in AI, showing how AI takes the human contribution higher, to assist decision-making, with creativity and innovating. These developments have immense chances of making a difference altogether in fields like health, education, and industry by rather increasing efficiency and productivity.

With great power, however, comes great responsibility. The ethical concerns in AI development and implementation certainly cannot be overlooked. Fairness, transparency, accountability, and privacy should be ensured in moving forward with size. Regulatory and governance frameworks will have to evolve to keep up with technological change if AI is to serve the greater good without infringing on the rights of the individual. Such challenges can only be overcome through interdisciplinarity. Having drawn experts from many diverse fields, more holistic and robust solutions are obtained that are not only ethically sound but technologically advanced. On the contrary, looking at AI combined with new technologies opens quite right interesting prospects in the future but requires a careful consideration of opportunities and risks. This book, basically, then sets out to inform readers about the dynamics at play between the mind and the machine. Embracing lessons learned earlier and developing a collaborative and ethical approach toward the development of Artificial Intelligence will allow us to unlock its full potential for the good of humanity and help us shape a better future.

Made in the USA
Monee, IL
04 November 2026

67379252R00105